Beginners Witch Guide to Hoodoo & Folk Magick

Gain Mastery in Rootwork, Conjure, and Spells with Roots, Herbs, Candles & Oils to Rid Negativity and Manifest Anything You Desire

Written By:
Glinda Porter

Table of Contents

Introduction 1

Part I: Understanding the Basics....................... 7

    What is Hoodoo? 8

    Principles 18

    A Relationship with Your Ancestors 24

    Working Altars 39

    Your Practice + the Elements of Hoodoo 46

    Hoodoo Roots... 55

    Seeds, Roots, Barks, Leaves, and Herbs....... 62

    Waters 81

    Cleansing Oils... 83

Part II: Spells, Tricks, and Rituals 85

    Preparing to Work with Roots......................... 85

    Mojo Bags... 99

    Magic Candles 115

    Using a Lamp... 116

    Foot Track Magick 117

    Spiritual Cleansing 120

    Cleansing Rituals and Spirit Washes 124

    Fires, Candles, and Incense Rites 144

    For Spell Casting 147

Spells for Keeping the Peace 154

Spells for Attraction, Love, and Relationships 165

Spells for Money, Luck, Abundance, and Prosperity 177

Spells for Success 185

Spells for Justice 194

Spells for Protection 203

Part III: Eradication and Getting Professional Help 211

Unhexing, Banishing, and Eradication Work 212

The End: Putting It All Together 239

Start Communicating 239

Get Organized 241

Get Cleaning 242

Get Focused 244

Keep Going 246

Introduction

Like nature and the four elements, magick is all around us. We use it every day in ways we're not even conscious of. A cup of tea that helps you to feel calm is a form of magic. Same with telling yourself the same stories over and over again or wearing the color red to entice arousal in a mate.

Think I'm exaggerating? Take a look at the advertisements on Instagram or YouTube. Corporations that advertise on these platforms work very hard to occupy space in your mind.

Everything these companies do is done with intent (which will be an important word, as we'll cover in later chapters); from the music they use to colors and fonts.

If you want clearer evidence of magick in everyday life, look no further than some of their logos. In the magical realm, symbolism is considered a graphic depiction of what the magician wants. Logos are symbols, in some cases they are sigils.

They act as a graphical way for a company or organization to remain present in the minds of the people.

This is one way magick is used on us, though most people remain unaware. You may be surprised to know that you are also using magick on yourself. You use intent every day, even if that intent is not conscious.

This is why I believe it is important to study magic. With knowledge you can better use your power to create the life you want, not do what a corporation wants you to do or be subject to your old habits.

There are countless magical traditions, but by picking this book, you've clearly shown an interest in hoodoo. And hopefully, that budding interest comes with an open mind.

One of the first things you should know is this tradition has many different names: aka rootwork, folk magick or magick, or simply work. Practitioners will describe what they do as 'working', 'a working', or 'doing work'.

A simpler (and perhaps controversial) way to put it is 'casting a spell', however this isn't all hoodoo is. We'll get into that in the next chapter. For the sake of simplicity, we'll refer to this practice as either conjure or hoodoo.

You might be wondering what the term 'rootwork' has to do with hoodoo. In short, roots are *extremely* important, not just in magic, but in hoodoo specifically.

This is a tradition that has its source in spiritual practices from African cultures that were ravaged by the slave trade. It is in these cultures that we discover the source of many of the things hoodoo practitioners do, for example, divination, chanting (or reciting mantras), and channeling.

If you think of roots as a metaphor, the connection becomes clear. Rootwork is a way for the millions of people whose ancestors were displaced by slavery to stay connected to their roots.

Over time, hoodoo evolved to incorporate practices from Native American and European cultures, as well as Christianity and Judaism. In some aspects, there were similarities between African cultures and Christianity. In many cases, disguising rootwork practices in Christianity became a matter of life and death for slaves.

The reason for the development of hoodoo was a desire to change one's life, specifically in the face of being enslaved. It came out of a need to survive, to have autonomy.

In short, this *work* is about putting your power back in your hands, literally.

In this book, we'll cover the basics—what conjure is and what it is not; the balance, history, core elements and principles. These first chapters are short, compared to what we could cover, but they're meant to give you information so you can start your research—this book is not meant to be a complete survey of the origins of conjure.

Of course, you don't *have* to study the basics. You are free to flip to the chapter on spells for attraction and start buying your materials right away, but you would just be doing yourself a disservice.

Often, this is why people gravitate towards a magical tradition like hoodoo. They need a job or want a way to create peace in the home and discover a spell that can help. But without knowing what they're really doing, they often experience results that are different than expected.

They get a job with a boss who is impossible to work with, for example. But instead of leaving and finding another job, they stick it out and try to force things to change because this was the job they *worked* (in the hoodoo sense) for.

Moreover, because hoodoo worked the first time, they'll be convinced of its effectiveness, and then stuck on a path of going back, again and again, to try to change a situation that is doomed.

Without knowing the core concepts -- or *root*s of root magick -- you set yourself up for going down a path of anger and frustration that may last years.

Your roots are perhaps the most important to consider as you embark on incorporating hoodoo into your life. Yes, I do mean your ancestors, but I am also using the word as a metaphor. Again, I use roots here to mean the roots in your mind, in your thinking.

If you think of your life as a plant, you've got the part that you can see; your experience in life, the money you make, your job, and relationships. Then you have your roots. The subconscious part of your mind that is creating your experience every day, moment by moment.

When you use hoodoo without understanding your roots, you can get what you want but your subconscious mind will often produce results that may be completely different than what you expect.

Everyone talks about examples of people who have won the lottery and lose all of their money within a couple years. Often the culprit is a scarcity mindset.

The same thing could be said of the person from the previous example, the one who got a job they won't quit. If they have the mindset that they won't be able to find another job (another example of scarcity thinking), they will be more inclined to stay in a situation that is unhealthy.

There are many practitioners who believe hoodoo is about you and your spirituality. It is a spiritual practice, not a religious one. This means you are free to worship according to your religion, if you so choose.

A spiritual practice is what will help you tend to your mental roots and get the results you expect with hoodoo.

To be successful, you need faith. Any fear, especially related to money or love, will mess with your results.

My intent with this book is to give you a basis upon which to begin your own journey in hoodoo. You'll quickly discover as you read that, same with the work of improving yourself, the research never ends.

This is why having what's called a 'beginner's mind' would do you well, especially after years have passed and you gain more and more knowledge. That's one of the great things about being an actual beginner—you have this covered.

Part I: Understanding the Basics

Many of our everyday practices can have magical uses. Taking a shower, organizing your files and workspace, cooking, working, exercising, even using the bathroom. Anything and everything can have a hoodoo application, if you're willing to get creative and open your mind.

You could say hoodoo is everywhere. A basic concept in hoodoo is paying respect to the things we can and cannot see. It is a way to connect, work with, and respect the powerful natural forces and world around us, and the forces that remain unseen to the naked eye.

By natural forces, I mean the earth: plants, trees, herbs, and dirt. More specifically, actual roots from plants, trees, and herbs. Common roots you will hear of are: High John the Conqueror, Mandrake, Licorice, and Angelica.

Unseen forces are exactly that: unseen. The air is often mentioned as an example of a force that we can't see but one we know exists. The same could be said of WIFI.

When it comes to hoodoo, we're talking about forces that are a little easier to deny. What our ancestors knew was (and is) that the spirit world is just as "real" as our 3D world. Colonizers saw how they lived, how close they were to Spirit, and immediately labeled it as evil.

Unfortunately, this mindset spread and eventually it wasn't the colonizer saying working with spirits was 'evil'; it was the descendants of our ancestors.

You may have encountered people who think like this in your life. If you want to build your practice, you have to give yourself permission to see things differently.

What is Hoodoo?

In simple terms, hoodoo is a magical and spiritual practice that emerged out of a need. 'Work' is an important word. You do work, and you find what works to achieve what you want.

Hoodoo is a practice that is about creating a change in our internal and external worlds. This is done through a series of methods that have been passed down for centuries.

Later on in this book we'll cover specifics, but for now know that these changes are signaled by using items such as oils, mojo bags, altars, (actual) roots, lights, candles, waters, colognes, herbs, and much, much more.

One thing that trips up many who are new to the practice is the use of biblical concepts and verses in conjure. This goes back to the influence of Christianity, as I mentioned in the introduction. This influence cannot be understated. To disguise what they were doing, many African slaves were able to practice their magick as long as slave owners thought they were practicing Christianity.

This goes back to hoodoo being about a balance between physical and non-physical worlds. When working with spirits, we approach from the perspective that we're working with the people who paved the way for us, often from hundreds and thousands of years back.

When we engage with hoodoo, we are engaging with ancestors whose lives centered around the church, whether Christian or Catholic.

This isn't to say that you need to memorize your bible verses in order to practice hoodoo, but it is a component that shouldn't come as a surprise to you when you come across a prosperity working that requires you to recite Psalms 72, for example.

If you have negative perceptions when it comes to the bible or talking about God, it's at this point when you have to decide if you're willing to put them aside so you can get serious about this practice.

This goes back to what I said earlier about respecting forces that are seen and unseen. We may not be able to understand the significance of the bible in this practice, but reverence to our ancestors is more important here than our personal preferences or histories.

For some, knowing this is all it takes. They're able to throw out all of their old ideas about Christianity. It's beautiful to see their relationship with God transform through a new perspective. None of this can happen, however, without willingness. Only you can decide if the sacrifice is worth it.

Let's look at a simple spell a beginning hoodoo practitioner may use to draw in money.

They work from home, in an apartment building, so this becomes the obvious place to focus on when doing the working. They start with a cleanse, during the waning moon, by removing items that they haven't used for years. Over this process, they tell themselves that they're cleaning out all of the old ideas they have about money and wealth.

As a last step to the cleaning, they use a floor wash that is made with things they have on hand: thyme, licorice root, Florida Water, frankincense essential oil, and holy water (that they made themselves, their belief being the most important ingredient).

After cleansing they bury nine coins in a plant on their balcony and cover it with dirt from a local bank. Throughout the working, she's praying and repeating her petition. She's also keeping her vibration high by *knowing* that what she's doing will produce results. After she's done, she watches her mindset for leftovers from the old ideas she'd cleansed out.

The physical things she used included the herbs and roots, the oil, the holy water, coins, the plant, and dirt.

The nonphysical things she used were the spirits of each item. The spirit of the thyme, licorice root, Florida Water, frankincense, and the holy water. Make no mistake: these spirits are where the power is contained. This is where hoodoo works.

In addition to recognizing the spirit of the roots and plants, the conjurer in our example made a point to pay attention to the unseen forces within *herself*. She didn't just do the working and go back to the same thoughts and ideas about money she had before. She could use the physical act of cleaning her space to stand in as a metaphor for a non-physical act, cleansing her mind of poverty thinking. This is another example of how magick blends the physical and non-physical worlds to create change in a person's life.

Before you put a list together of items to buy and whip out a credit card, there are some basics when it comes to hoodoo that you must have secured prior to doing your first working. We'll cover this in the coming chapters.

Striking a Balance

We know what some say about magick already: that it's evil, that it spawns from the devil, it's a sin, and it should be abolished. On the other side of that, what is considered being 'good'? It doesn't take much to imagine what that is like. Many of us know this intimately.

Maybe you made the mistake of sharing your enthusiasm with the wrong person.

It doesn't have to even be magic, unfortunately too many of us know the pain that comes with sharing our happiness with someone else who lashes out in anger, thereby making us and the things we love "wrong".

Ironically, this negative mindset was responsible for eradicating the same practices that many of us are now trying to reconnect with, via conjure.

If you have experienced negative reactions to your spirituality, you may have already learned an important lesson about secrecy. As you build your practice and gather your materials, you'll know to keep your work to yourself. Or another way to put it: you'll know who you can talk to and who to keep your work secret from.

This is one of the many truths of conjure. In this world, you will find support and scorn, depending on where you look. You can share your enthusiasm for the abilities you always knew you had with someone else, maybe another person reading this book, and you will find someone else who is also discovering their power and is just as excited as you are.

However, tell the wrong person that you are reading this book, and get a very different reaction. This is the reason I kept my tarot cards and candles hidden as a teenager.

It's also the reason why the best response when encountering people who have negative things to say about your practice is silence.

I am using this fact of magick to make a point about balance in the world of conjure. We have this idea that there is "good" magick and "bad" magic, thanks to Hollywood. People who work bad magick wear a lot of black and dark colors. They are evil, hungry for power, or acting out some lifelong revenge plot.

In reality, the concept of 'good vs. evil' has no real place in magic. It depends on how *you* look at it. Once you decide there's a type of magick or intent that is 'good', you've created 'bad' magic. But these rules are your own. Even if they are passed on to you by someone who claims to have some expertise that you don't have, their ideas aren't real for you unless you decide to make them real. If this sounds like the law of attraction, that's because it is.

Thinking of magick in terms of good and evil will *not* keep "evil" magic away from you. It will do the opposite. You will see evidence of 'evil' magic. You'll also be more likely to criticize or label other people's practices. Keep in mind, this labeling of what others do is no different than how colonizers criticized traditional African cultures and spirituality.

So, what does balance mean when we're talking hoodoo?

Many things.

The reason why it's important to remove any thoughts of 'good' vs. 'evil' magick is because these ideas only cause you harm. We all have light and dark within us. What we tend to label 'evil' is that dark side, our shadow self.

This is the part of us that we try to hide from ourselves and from the world. I keep mentioning money and lack mindsets, but the truth is this is where a lot of people struggle with their shadow.

Let's look at an example people may be familiar with: hating wealthy people. What some will not admit is that their hate for rich people stems from jealousy at not being able to live the life they want to live. What's underneath that is deep pain and feelings of despair and fear.

One of the reasons many workers will tell new conjurers to do shadow work is because you can curse yourself with these unexamined emotions of fear, jealousy, envy, or hate.

Even if you do all of your shadow work, you will still have a shadow. That is the nature of being a human. If you accept that your shadow is always there. Within you light and dark both exist and owning this opens you up to your full power.

The truth is, you have the ability to bless and to curse. This is what practitioners call being able to work with both hands, or being a 'two-headed worker'.

Think of what happens in nature when a plant is uprooted, or a weed is pulled: new growth happens in its place. Everything in nature, in life, happens in balance. You seeing evidence of a world you create in your mind is a form of this balance. Another way to put that is, as within so without.

When we as conjurers use plants and roots for our magic, we're taking and using the energy and spirits of that plant for our own purposes. You could use these powers without any reverence at all, but then you are not practicing hoodoo to its full power. When we talk about balance in conjure or hoodoo, we're talking about a give and take relationship.

You might read that and think: *what do I have to give to spirit?*

Approaching hoodoo from the perspective that you don't have anything to offer is another example of poverty thinking. Do everything you can to wipe that idea from your mind because it is simply false. Many of us think that what we have to offer is limited by the money in our bank account. This is another example.

Every thought you have, every place you put your energy in now, whether that is in studying to improve your craft or scrolling through Instagram, is a "payment" of sorts.

Of course, actual money is a form of payment as well, and some spirits will accept this as an offering, but I'm willing to bet that if you were able to get your hands on this book, you already have an abundance of ways you can give back to spirit to show your gratitude.

You might be wondering who your thoughts pay. The answer goes back to unseen forces, or the presence of spirit in our lives, and the idea that we are helped in countless ways by these forces. What many fail to see is how poverty thinking results in more poverty thinking. What's really happening is, the spirits fed by a poverty mindset grow; much like the wolf in the Cherokee legend. This spirit grows in balance to how much you feed the mindset.

This same concept is applied to roots, and if we want to work with roots to change our lives, then we must work to give as much as we take.

We also want to provide a clear channel for change to happen by doing the work on ourselves to remove blockages. Shadow work never ends. Healing is a journey that continues even after death, so there is no being 'done' with your dark side. You use your awareness to work with your shadow.

Principles

Respect for Ancestors

Who are we working with when we practice? Who are the spirits that help us on the other side? Who helps us in ways we can't see or recognize?

Our ancestors.

You might not know who your ancestors are by name, but they know who you are. Reverence to those who have worked hard so we can live the way we live is a core principle of hoodoo practice.

We've talked a bit about respecting the herbs and roots you use for workings. I bring it up here to emphasize a core principle of respecting the natural forces in and around your environment.

You personally have countless ancestors, in the thousands. The spirit of the men and women who came before you are with you now, in your blood and bones.

Each person you are connected to had to survive the physical harshness of life. They had to live in societies that tried to wipe out their livelihoods and beat their spirit down. They fought in wars. They worked and worked just to get the opportunity to pursue a better life in another country and had to make decisions that you and I could never fathom.

Somewhere deep down, you know all of these stories because a part of you *lived* these stories. And I'm not just talking about past lives.

When I think about everything my ancestors went through, I take all of the hurt, anger, and despair and commit to living my life in peace, love, joy, and abundance in hard and in easy times.

In my personal relationship with those who have paved my way, I know that this is what they want for my life.

It took some time for me to be able to listen to the voice of my ancestors, and to be confident that they were with me in the first place. I'm guessing that you weren't raised in a home where it was common to talk to ancestors, and if my guess is correct, then you and I have this in common.

I started my relationship with three things: an open heart, a sincere desire that went beyond curiosity, and respect.

Respect for Environment

Hoodoo is a practice that looks different, depending on which region you are in. New Orleans is probably the most notable example of this. You might not have a hoodoo practice specific to where you live, but what I want you to take from this is you and your environment come first.

You might find a working online that asks for Angelica root, but if this is hard to find in your region, this is something you need to be aware of at least. Most of us are lucky to live in countries where anything we want is accessible, if we're willing to pay the shipping.

You'll also want to be mindful of going out and picking fresh flowers and plants. This is knowing what plants grow natively in your region, what trees and plants are endangered and which ones thrive. This might require getting another book to research botanicals, but if you're serious about this practice then you don't need much convincing.

Pine is easy enough to find, depending on where you are. If the working you're preparing for calls for this plant, it's always better to go out and find it in nature rather than buying it. Keeping the principle of respect in mind, you want to know the specific varieties of pine growing close to you and information about the plant if you're going to use it in a spell.

Before ripping a branch off of a tree, speak to the tree, the roots, and show your gratitude. One of the ways I do this is by cleaning up any garbage I find in wooded areas in my neighborhood. However, you don't have to do this just when you're looking for something for a working.

For example, pine trees are a resilient plant species that can survive through harsh winters. It's commonly used for cleansing, protection, healing, and in some cases exorcisms. Because this tree is native to North America, it is likely that you'll find some use for it in your workings. What kind of pine grows in your neighborhood?

A bit of research will tell you Sugar Pine, for example, is considered 'king', and has a sap that was used by some Native Americans as a sweetener. This is information you can find on Wikipedia. Knowing this, you might pray to the Sugar Pine plant and ask that it add its sweetness to a cleansing, a nice touch if you're using it in a wash for your home.

Respect for Self

Louisa was ready to start working conjure, but knew she had some work to do. As a child, she witnessed domestic violence in the home and even though those years were long gone, it was difficult for her to release some of the patterns she'd learned.

Somewhere in her late teens she started to believe that her life was an aberration.

Thinking this way didn't feel right, but it helped her to stay small, and in that it helped her to survive. As she got older, the idea became less about survival and more about staying inside the small life she'd created in her mind.

Initially, Louisa came to hoodoo for money problems. As you can probably guess, she was heavy in debt and never seemed to make enough to get by. But in our consultation, I told her that if she continued with this mindset, she would never be released from her struggles.

Even if we found a working that drew in the money she was looking for, without tending to her roots she would be stuck in a cycle. It would be better for her to deal with what she thought and felt about herself first.

The good thing about my meeting with Louisa (and I have changed her name to protect her identity) is that she had awareness of what her issue was and had a strong desire to be honest. This is a power, one that she had to acknowledge was sharpened like a knife over her childhood.

As an adult, she has learned to accept her own darkness for what it is. She also had to accept how uncomfortable she was with the concept of having power. Her ego was wrapped up in the idea that she was weak and powerless to change her life.

But to change her financial condition, she had to accept the power she had over her experience of love, security, and money.

She also had to accept that the thoughts she had would show up in both her physical and spiritual worlds. Otherwise, the workings done would be out of balance, she would be working with spirits that serve her old mindset.

Nothing can happen in the physical world that doesn't appear in the spiritual. Balance is one of the core principles of hoodoo.

A Relationship with Your Ancestors

Get into your history; who your people are. This is the place that you need to start at the beginning of your hoodoo practice.

Q: What if my ancestors didn't believe in magic?

This is a great question. If you've heard negative things about magick from your parents or grandparents, it's reasonable to deduce that these ideas were passed down to them. It follows, then, that your ancestors may not appreciate your efforts to become better at a practice they didn't believe in.

Here's what I would say: first, when a person passes on, they leave behind their physical body and other aspects of the human experience. They literally get to see life for what it truly is (if they want to).

Have you ever visited or seen a medium speak to someone who has passed on? More often, these spirits send messages to their loved ones that demonstrate that after passing, their perspective on life and the things that happened while they were on earth has changed.

The way we think is one of the things that we can leave behind once our spirit goes beyond this plane of existence.

This isn't to say that your ancestors gained a new perspective of magick once they died. I can't say that, I don't know you and I don't know your people. The only way you can begin to figure out what they felt is to ask them.

There is a chance that once they passed on, their perspective changed. This is one of the reasons it is important for you, in your home and in your practice, to build a relationship with your ancestors.

Here's where your prayers and inner knowing come in. What do I mean by this? All-day, every day, if you wake up and have life in you, you are repeating things to yourself. They might not be full sentences, but you're feeling some kind of emotion. You are creating a vibration. This vibration is a form of prayer or talking to yourself.

Rev. Ike (who could have been a hoodoo practitioner, we will never know) says it best: *God is thought*. We all know the sayings: 'thoughts are things' and 'life and death lie in the power of your own tongue'.

If your mood has ever changed because of what someone else said or did, that is a demonstration of this power.

You can use this power to communicate with your ancestors right now by thanking them for everything they've done to bring you to this point in your life.

Connecting with Your Benevolent Ancestors

Here's another truth: we all have ancestors in our bloodline who would not be supportive of what we're doing to improve our lives. They are just like the people we encounter every day. By the same token, we all have ancestors who are eager to support us in whatever we want to do.

The way to connect with these ancestors is to simply ask, using the power of your thought and your words.

A simple prayer might include the following:
1. A statement of gratitude to your ancestors for bringing you to this point in your life, and for the things they do that you may not be aware of.
2. Affirming your overall intent; what you're looking to do. With this, you may want to state that you will keep your heart and mind open to their messages.
3. What you need help with, or why you're approaching your ancestors.
4. Acknowledgment of the things you're looking to sacrifice or banish in your life now (if applicable).
5. A request that your benevolent ancestors come to your aid and show you the way.

You can close this prayer the same way it was opened: with thanks. After praying, it's up to you to stay open to their communication. I'm going to assume that this listening is something you're somewhat familiar with, even as a beginner. It's the same kind of listening you do when dancing or creating art, it's hearing with your "good" ear.

Listening

Many feel some confusion when practicing this kind of listening because it is easy to block it out and think you are making it all up by yourself.

It might help for me to share what it feels like when I'm listening, especially when I was just starting out on my hoodoo journey. My mind was overrun with negative thinking, even in the smallest ways. So, whenever something very positive or uplifting came to me, I knew that was the voice of God speaking through my higher self.

This is where communication with my ancestors started. The channel was open, you could say. The more I was able to hear the voice of God, the more I could attune myself to the voice of my ancestors. The differences are very slight, but subtlety is the nature of communication with God.

It might be the same for you or slightly different, depending on your openness, and how comfortable you are with receiving communication.

As you open up, you'll also improve at hearing your own voice; the voice of your ego. Maybe on reading those last few sentences you thought that I must be "better" at communicating with God than you are. A Course in Miracles would call this a 'trick of the ego'.

Hearing the Ego

Once you start to listen, you cannot avoid hearing. You are strengthening your sensitivity and attuning yourself to more and more subtle forms of communication. I struggled with this myself: the more I got quiet and listened, the more I heard things I didn't want to hear.

The more you learn to listen to the voice of your own ego, the more you'll hear it speak to you in patterns. One common pattern that all of us know is statements around an idea that sounds like "I'm not good enough". Thinking someone else is "better" than you at something, like talking to spirit, is an example of this type of thinking.

The benevolent ancestors you call on can help with hearing their voice over your own as well. Again, the only thing you need to do is ask. If it sounds like I'm talking about capital-s Spirit, that is on purpose. Your benevolent ancestors are connected with Spirit, with Infinite Love, Infinite Abundance, Infinite Wisdom.

It's this connection that will help you live in balance and maintain that balance in your hoodoo and conjure work.

Another mindset that we're quick to shift to, especially as we consider solving our problems with magic, is that we are stupid for having the problems we have in the first place, that the minor things we're dealing with are too small or insignificant for these mighty powers.

You guessed it: this is another trick!

'Big' vs. 'Small' Problems

Even if you don't know how they're going to help you or you feel like your problems are too small, take them to your ancestors.

I would say that as a beginner, you *want* to take the problems you think are small to your ancestors. Chances are you'll find those small problems are connected to bigger ones, so doing this is a way to ease into your practice.

And eventually, you will discover there are no 'big' problems and 'small' problems when it comes to Spirit.

Like dividing magick into 'good' and 'evil', this concept of complicated problems is self-made. Thinking a problem is big gives you a reason to feel like it cannot be solved, and that way of thinking curses you to continuously search for answers and solutions outside of yourself.

This might be the reason you decided to begin practicing hoodoo for yourself. If you've gone to practitioners over and over again, you already know what it feels like to think your problems are bigger than you are. It's a trap many have fallen into.

The problems you are approaching hoodoo to solve were created by you. As big as you think they are, you are bigger. Before working, you *must* know this and believe it.

You must believe in the power of your ancestors. You must know the power of your ancestors flows through you and contributes to your power. Use this thought to replace any belief you have in the power of your problems.

You might wonder why you have to change your perspective on your problems if you're taking them to your ancestors. The question really is: where is your faith? In some ways, having faith in yourself and in your ancestors (by way of God) is the same. In a way, this goes back to the section on hoodoo Principles: Respect for Self.

You have to believe God exists inside of you, so that the work you do can take effect because it is by your hands that you do this work. The work starts with you. If you don't believe in yourself, how can you believe your work is going to do what you want it to do?

If this isn't an idea you are comfortable with, then you can just focus on having faith in God and your ancestors. As your work becomes more and more successful, your faith in yourself will grow in proportion to your faith in God. In other words, your ancestors can take care of your lack of faith in yourself (as long as you remain open and willing)!

Building Your Altar

How great is it to know that all of your problems can be solved with the help of Spirit?

If you're beginning to feel some gratitude in knowing this, try to bottle up this feeling. Gratitude is the vibration you want to conjure and maintain when building your altar.

An altar is the physical manifestation of your relationship with your ancestors, and a non-negotiable for the serious hoodoo practitioner.

This is a place for you to speak to and receive messages from your ancestors, a place to present your offerings and to do your work. It is a kind of a spiritual center for your home. You can also keep specific types of altars in your space for your working.

Some practitioners have multiple altars; they keep one specifically for their ancestors, another for working (which we'll get into later). An altar for money, one for love, the list goes on.

Do not worry if you don't have the space for all of this. The point is to have a dedicated area for your work. Altars can take different forms, but a basic altar set up usually has:

- a bible,
- at least one candle,
- water in a wine glass or other glass,
- images of your ancestors, and
- items belonging to your ancestors, such as jewelry.

Usually, this is set up with a white tablecloth atop a table. You will find altars as different and varied as there are homes.

Other basics include food. This is usually cooked or baked, it's always better if you know what foods your ancestors preferred and take the time to prepare and offer what you know they like. You can also include your tarot cards or anything you use for divination, images, or any depictions you have of deities that mean something to you.

You don't want to keep food on your altar for too long. When drinks or food get cold, dispose of it. If you were to offer your ancestors an afternoon cup of tea, for example, in the evening you dispose of it at your front door. Or if you don't want to make a mess of your hallway, find a tree and pour it out there. This is how you dispose of food left on your altar as well; never throw out or put food in the compost.

Offerings can be left as often as you like, but try to ritualize this, for example leaving food once a week.

The table in your home can take any form. It might be built-in, like by a bay window or shelf. If you have more space, you can go bigger and use a small desk or table that has a dedicated spot in your home.

It's most important to set up an altar that works for you. This might mean creating an altar that doesn't *appear* like one at first glance. Or it might mean that you use a smaller table that can fit perfectly in a corner.

This space is and will become sacred. It should be out of the way of anyone touching it, other than you. Do not feel obligated to tell anyone what it is or why any of the items are on it. If it seems too many people are interacting with the space, you may want to move it to somewhere more private.

Once the altar is built, do a small ritual where you call on your ancestors. The main purpose of this is to present your altar space to them so that they know this is their physical home in your life, a representation of the home they have in your heart and mind.

Getting Prepared

You need a way to get calm and centered. Not just for this ritual, but for everything. You do not want to begin this ritual with *any* anxiety at all. Maybe you've never done this before, but remove any jitters or feelings of being 'freaked out'. Unsure is fine, but try to convert that unsure feeling to reverence.

Do something that tells your mind this is a special moment. One simple way to do this is to get dressed up; wear all white or something that marks what you're doing.

Prepare what you are going to present as offerings to your ancestors. A few ideas: coins, warm food, a drink you know they liked (though wine, rum, or whiskey will suffice), fresh flowers, coffee or tea (with sugar), coins, bread or fruit that has been cut and is ready to eat. If you leave a food, like nuts or seeds, leave it open (i.e. not in a bottle or jar that's closed).

The last thing you want to have on hand is your prayers and a bible, either physical or digital to read from (unless you have what you want to recite memorized).

Your prayers will require some thought beforehand, depending on how formal you want to be. If you're more comfortable just talking to your ancestors like a friend, do that.

Opening the Ritual

Open the ritual by anointing yourself and your space with a hoodoo oil. There are many ways to anoint yourself, but here's a simple method using your body's pressure points and third eye.

1. Set your intention (i.e. Say aloud something like: *Thank you, [your name for God] for facilitating my connection to my ancestors.*). Continue to repeat your intention throughout as you apply oil to your pressure points:
2. Apply a drop of the oil to one wrist and rub your wrists together, then apply oil (take more as needed):
    a. The upper shell of your ear.
    b. Behind your shoulders.
    c. Your third eye.

Alternatively, if you don't have an oil or prefer not to use them on your skin, you can anoint with a spray or a cologne.

Do not worry about buying an oil or spray. These can be made with water and a few ingredients you probably already have in your kitchen. These instructions will be covered in Part 2, under Cleaning Rituals and Spirit Washes.

With sprays, you set and state your intention while spraying the air at least once. Three times is more than sufficient. The number of times you spray is important. Three represents a holy trinity.

After you've anointed, get the fire started: light your candle(s) and/or incense.

Make Your Offerings

If you're using smoke, run the items you're offering over and through the smoke to cleanse them and then 'present' them to your ancestors. This can be done by holding the item and then lifting it, as if you were giving a gift to someone much taller than you.

Do this act with your whole being. Imagine your benevolent ancestors coming around and graciously accepting what you offer.

Dial In

Read Psalms 23. If you don't have a bible, look the prayer up online. There are also many bible apps available for free and with no ads.

Call on your ancestors. Here's an example of what you might want to say. Feel free to edit or change according to your needs: *I now call on the benevolent and honored spirits of my lineage, every man and woman who sired and birthed the men and women who now live through me.*

I invite you into my home and into my life. This altar is where we will meet, and where I will offer my deep gratitude for the sacrifices you've made, and the work you continue to do on my behalf.

I offer you [name the items you've offered in the form of food, scents, items, etc.] with honor, love, and thanks. I hope they are pleasing to you.

You don't have to make the call super formal. I would actually recommend telling your ancestors that you're just starting on this journey, that this is the first time you are working with them (though there's a good chance they know already). You can also ask for guidance on your relationship with them. Be open to even the smallest ways that they speak to you.

Once you say that your altar is the place where you will meet and offer gratitude, you have to actually use your altar to meet your ancestors and offer gratitude when you get there. This ritual is about making a commitment to a relationship. What you say in this meeting is important, so take note.

Get Comfortable

Spend some time in silence, just listening. You may receive guidance on things you're dealing with right now. Or you may just feel feelings, like love, peace, or just a general good You Are Blessed feeling. Sit as long as you like. You will intuitively feel when your time at the altar is complete.

You don't just have to sit and listen, however. You can sing, read, and talk to your ancestors as if they were there with you. Share what is going on in your life right now. Be open to getting answers to questions you've been asking for years. This has happened to me and is not uncommon.

However, keep your expectations checked and clear. You may not get the answer you're looking for right away, but this might be because you are not ready for the answer. The most important thing to do here is stay open.

Close

I keep closings very simple at my altar. I simply clasp my hands, close my eyes, and feel gratitude throughout my body. This is my everyday practice, and since you're doing a first-time ritual at your altar, you may want to do something more formal.

Express gratitude. Even if you didn't "feel" anything, tell your ancestors that you're grateful for their presence.

Some practitioners will end rituals by putting out a candle or clapping once. These acts read more 'sending spirits away' to me. I prefer to use a large candle that I can burn for as long as I am at home.

As mentioned previously, food should not be kept on your altar for more than a week. And once you're ready to dispose of it, put it outside. Do not throw the food away.

In your practice, you'll come across countless more altar and ritual ideas, some you'll work, and others you'll let go by.

Working Altars

An ancestor altar is very common in hoodoo practice. In addition to this, you may want to create an altar specifically for a certain aspect of your life or something you want.

Here, I go over a few of these types of altars, and some ways you can get creative. With each, you want to think about how you can invite the presence of God and/or the Goddess (or Solar Light, whichever deity speaks to you). Your ancestor altar may have God in every aspect. Or you may use a candle to represent Solar Light.

Some altars are permanent, but if there's something specific you're working on, you could use a temporary altar.

The Self-Love Altar

If you've struggled with self-image issues or come from a childhood home where you witnessed violence, a self-love altar is a space to center and heal.

It's a place where you can take everything you love about yourself and honor it. This might require some creativity as you're taking intangible aspects and making them physical.

A candle on this altar could represent your inner light. And with the countless different types of candles you can get, you can really find something that speaks to *you* on a deep level.

The four elements are thought to stand in for aspects of life and living: earth honors your foundation, water your emotions and intuition, wind your thinking, and fire your willpower. These are common elements in all altars. You can use things that you like to represent these elements.

For example, if you love frogs, you could create a self-love altar that is heavy on the frog decor. If you're an artist, you could paint your self-love altar on a massive canvas. The advantage of this is it saves space in your home.

Small statues, trinkets, and figurines are great for altars in general, but especially for tapping into your personality and attributes. Animal and mystical symbolism is great for this. A horse, for example, could represent freedom, strength of spirit, triumph, and courage. A fairy could represent a sense of wonder and magic.

A trinket like a pair of glasses or binoculars could represent foresight. Jewelry, abundance and beauty. Crystals like rose quartz are great to represent love.

A figurine of a small Oscar award can be immensely powerful if you one day want to win an Oscar.

As you can tell, the possibilities for this kind of altar are endless. Searching options on Google is a great option, but you can also use tarot cards or think of things that just mean something to *you*. However, don't deny the power in common symbols, like stars. Many times, you can go to a local dollar store and find lots of usable stuff. Or you may already have something at home.

You are a strong spirit. A self-love altar is a space where you can honor your true spirit, regardless of how you've had to shift and bend to exist in the world.

The Money Altar

What's your relationship with money? How do you feel when you look at people who have more money than you? A money altar is a space to heal your relationship with money, if you need to, or honor the strong relationship you already have.

Many of us have the misperception that "no one will pay us the money we want". A money altar is an ideal place to heal this idea.

You can be creative with this altar, creativity is the channel through which money and abundance flows. The only rule is to keep the intent of the altar focused. Putting a random object on your money altar will muddy up the lines of communication.

Money is one of the first things you want on this type of altar. If you have any dollar bills or coins hanging around, especially if they're different denominations, use these. It doesn't matter how much or what denomination you have, even monopoly money will work if you want it to.

Old checks hanging around are *great* for a money altar. This is an idea from The Secret, but applies here. You might have a check from a closed bank account. Use these to start writing checks to yourself with amounts that you want. Write an infinity check!

The usual items for most altars apply for this type as well: crystals, candles, herbs, roots, and other items like money, oils, and dirt that we have and will cover.

Statues of deities that are associated with wealth and money are ideal for a money altar, for example, Oshun, or Fortuna.

Tarot cards work as well, though you may want to purchase a deck that is separate from the one you use for readings, or you can print out an image from online.

You want to think about things that mean something to you for your money altar. A growing plant can be a symbol of expansion. Watering a plant on your money altar every day can be important symbolism, same with pruning the plant and removing dead leaves (removing old ideas).

Pinecones or double samaras (those things that fall from trees in a pinwheel motion) are a symbol of abundance, if you live in an area where these things are everywhere.

The Deity Altar

Before building a deity altar, you want to have a clear idea of the deity you're building for. This seems like it goes without saying but having a deep relationship with a deity is key.

If you respect more than one deity, then you'll know whether you can use one altar for every deity or if you need one altar for each deity.

Some deities require their own space, so sharing their sacred space in your home is not an option.

You'll also want to know what the deity you're honoring likes to receive. Money is one example. It means something to us, and can work on your money altar, but some deities may not care for money at all.

One of the basics you'll want on the altar is a statue or some representation of the deity that the altar is being built for. Some altars will even include more than one statue or depiction. You want these visual elements to represent the deity for you, items that as soon as you come into contact with them, you connect with your deity.

Creating an Altar in Your Mind

This is an option to consider if you don't have space for an altar or aren't really interested in creating a physical space in your home, as described.

To Spirit, everything is energy. Our physical world helps us humans with that, but for spirit, these physical things don't mean much. This is why intent is so important. You can (and do) create a whole world in your mind and without intention, you can create a lot without being aware.

Creating an altar in your mind uses visualization, an important skill that some people find easier than others.

You can create a whole castle in your mind that is an altar, then speak to your ancestors and the spirits you are calling to let them know that space is for them. If you are unable to purchase or find the items for your altar, you can just imagine them. Or better yet, create them in your mind and place them in your mind altar.

The Choose Your Adventure Altar

Whereas there are specific rules for ancestors, you can create an altar for whatever you want to draw into your life. Remember how everything has a spirit? Creating an altar is basically honoring these spirits.

You can create an altar for style, peace, and serenity, beauty, a season, a career you want, good health, education, a sport, a craft, for a loving family, cooking, the elements, even a place, maybe somewhere you want to live, like a cottage or a farm.

Your Practice + the Elements of Hoodoo

Dipping your toes into hoodoo can seem daunting. With no familiarity with what it is and how it works, just finding a spell for you can be a challenge, especially when you are new to the practice.

If you have to work in secret from nosy friends and family, getting a package of 7-day candles, Florida water, and holy oils might not be so easy.

And that's not to mention the costs. There are the costs of buying what you need for a working and possibly the costs of setting up an altar.

As with everything, part of respecting your ancestors, your environment, and yourself, means doing your research and knowing what works for you. Copying spells from someone else is fine, but with your knowledge and knowing the core elements of hoodoo, you are better equipped to create your own workings.

If you know the core elements of hoodoo, this becomes easier with time. This is where we incorporate many of the topics we've covered already. In hoodoo, Spirit is at the core of everything. Practitioners think about the spirit of everything they work with, what is at the core or root.

1. Working with Spirit.
2. Working with Nature: Roots, plants, herbs.

3. Working with Water: Cleansing, purification, protection.
4. Working with Place: Graveyards, banks, churches, crossroads.
5. Working with the Mind: Balance and containment.

As mentioned, hoodoo exists to make your life easier. Do not burden yourself with getting supplies and materials that someone else says you need for a spell.

There is a way to practice with what's readily available to you. The things you already touch and experience every day can be used in your hoodoo. Plus, you probably already have some powerful herbs in your kitchen cabinets. Often items you have just hanging around as decor, like candles and seashells, can be used in your working.

Working with Spirit

Your day might start with a prayer acknowledging the ancestors and reconnecting with the work you're doing in your life. A practice could begin with acknowledging those who went before you and the power they lend to you.

If you don't have an image or any idea of who your ancestors are, this might seem like a challenge. This is one of the painful consequences of the slave trade; many descendants of ancestors living in North America don't have any connection to those who came before them.

Many of my clients know this pain intimately. Some of them come from families who just do not seem to care about their lineage, so their questions and quest for knowledge are met with indifference, if not anger.

Their blood still runs through your veins, and in this way, you will stay connected to them for as long as you are alive. Use the power of prayer and your words that we discussed in the previous chapter to start building the connection. You might not have names, but a desire and deep respect are all you need.

Keep going back to your altar and keep working at building these relationships. Here are some methods you can start using immediately as part of your practice:

1. Visit your altar every morning and say *good morning!* to your ancestors. In The hoodoo Altar, I'll talk about how you can create an altar in your mind if you don't have access to your physical space.
2. Make offerings every week of food, flowers, jewelry, money, or other 'special' items. Do not half-step with this. Give full bottles of alcohol if you choose to give alcohol, clean money, fresh flowers, and fresh food.

3. Clean your altar regularly. Add cleaning your altar to your regular home cleanings. Or align cleanings with moon cycles.
4. Go to your altar throughout the day to offer your own energy; sing if you can, offer gratitude, say a prayer, some thanks. Go to your altar throughout the day if something troubles you or you have questions. Get into the habit of going to your altar, even if you don't have something physical to give.

Working with Nature

The term 'rootwork' is interchangeable with hoodoo. Other than roots, natural elements, such as herbs, plants, seeds, leaves, peels, and dirt play an important role in hoodoo practice. Take any vegetable or plant you have or that grows around you.

An orange can feed your body, but the peel can also be used in working for luck and money. Same with fennel seeds and bay leaves.

Each of the natural powers we use in hoodoo pulled their power in from the earth. Not only does the earth power the growth of the plants and herbs you use, but it also powers our own growth. It feeds us every day and grounds us in place, even as we run around and get distracted with living life.

Often, we get so enthusiastic about a spell, we're looking around to find a store that sells everything in one place. Before buying roots and herbs was a possibility, conjurers either grew what they used on their own, or got what they needed straight from the source: the earth.

If you can, try to forage what you need or grow it on your own. This might mean doing a few substitutions here and there, and if you choose to use an alternate ingredient, be careful to understand what results you might get with what you're using.

Working with Waters

I'm using 'waters' here as a metaphor for cleansing and purification. Your energy is affected by countless things on any given day. Our world continuously bombards us with all types of ideas that can either zap our energy or empower us.

Let's be honest, we're more likely to be drawn to the things that zap our energy.

Need I list examples? The news, social media, gossip YouTube channels, reality television, trauma fiction. Going out and having a negative interaction with someone on the street or in a grocery store is a prime example of the kind of interaction that can muck up your energy.

Of course, we'd all like to think we're immune to the energy of others, but even with a strong mental and vibrational shield, most people need to continuously keep their field maintained.

In this way, your spirit is a lot like your physical body. It requires work to keep healthy and in tune. As sensitive people, we are open to absorbing negative energies that need to be removed regularly.

We'll talk more about cleansing in another section, but for now, know that within hoodoo there are various liquids; oils, colognes, perfumes, spiritual waters, and vinegars that are used for multiple purposes. There are money drawing oils, two types of Florida Water, war and peace water, and Four Thieves Vinegar, for example.

Working with Place

Spirit is everywhere. Have you ever walked into a place and noticed that it just *felt* different? Some would call this a "vibe", short for vibration. You feel this when you walk into someone's home, but types of places have the same effect.

Think about what it feels to walk into a school, a library, or a bodega. Each of these places has a distinct vibe to it that you know but don't think about too much.

Graveyards and crossroads are two important places in hoodoo because of the energy they carry. Other places that you'll often hear or read about in your research are banks and churches.

Specifically, you'll most often work with the spirit of a place like a bank by using the dirt from the land around where it is located (if it's surrounded by concrete, that is another story). You could really get creative with this but using dirt from just anywhere could produce unintended results.

The symbolism of crossroads is also big in conjure. The crossroads represent many things. In our plane of existence, we live in a world where we can experience both 3D life and the spirit world.

Working with the Mind

Just like the spaces in our 'real' world that have special meanings in hoodoo, there are some mental concepts that conjurers give reverence to. Another way to put it, is there are definite hoodoo laws.

One example we've touched on previously is the law of *balance*. You could say this is a law that rules our lives, but, as we know, in hoodoo this concept is respected on a different level.

Look around your life and within right now. Can you find examples of places where there is perfect balance? What does that look and feel like? What does it look and feel like when things are out of balance?

It's easy enough to pick these out because the situations that you came to hoodoo for are probably the same ones that are out of balance. This is how we know that things are out of balance: we feel it. It's obvious in many ways, and it's often very uncomfortable. You see this often in the workplace.

There always seems to be one person who is less than qualified for the job they're doing, which means the other people on their team (if we're honest, it's usually one person) is left picking up the slack.

The person or people who have to work more than what they usually would are then out of balance within themselves: they're working more than they're being paid for. This is fertile ground to trigger emotional imbalance as well. Often when we see the words 'emotional imbalance', we go straight to depression, but here I'm talking about emotions like resentment, anger, and jealousy.

Imbalance also highlights the next concept, *containment*. When things get out of balance, it tends to affect other areas that most times are never even considered. In the example above, co-workers are less effective in their own work because they're distracted by the extra weight they have to carry.

This is a simple example of the concept of containment in action. In the above example, we're explicitly talking about boundaries. But many magical traditions use this concept. In the hoodoo tradition, one example of containment is in workings like mojo bags or nation sacks.

Here, the power of spirit is concentrated and contained within a vessel for use in whatever way directed by the working.

Before planning your spell, you want to understand exactly what is out of balance so the work you do is applied (or contained) with specificity.

Mind practices:
1. Take a moment each day to practice stillness. Some people would call this 'meditation' and if that works for you, then work it.
2. Say 'I don't know' more. This might sound or seem simplistic, but don't think of this as pretending to be stupid. Our egos like to convince us we know everything. This practice is about opening up and working your beginner's mind.

Hoodoo Roots

In its earliest days, hoodoo was called many different things. One of the terms for healing that the first conjurers practiced was called 'rootwork', 'mojo', 'conjure', 'folk magick', or 'mojo'.

There are also different names for magickal practices similar to hoodoo. For example, what's known as hoodoo in the United States would be called 'obeah' in Jamaica.

Rootwork

We used to use plants for healing. Many indigenous cultures still do. One of the more common ways plants are still used in this way is with teas. You probably have a selection of teas in your kitchen cabinet right now that can be used for one purpose or another.

Take some time to research the different dried flowers in your teas and what their magical correspondences are. Having tea is really having dried flowers, which are dried plants. As we know, there is a lot of power in these plants.

You may discover that you already have a plant that will work for what you need, in the form of a tea.

To practice seriously, you'll need to do more than spend a few minutes researching. Smell the plants, herbs, and roots you have. Feel them. Look at them to know how they appear so you can tell one dried or fresh plant from the next.

You may already know the taste from cooking and drinking, but ideally you get to a point where you can tell a plant (and know its properties useful for your work) by looking at it.

Often beginning practitioners have a list of things they go out and buy for their first spell. While this is fine when it comes to working, hoodoo is about being connected to plants, roots, and herbs. It is the root in rootwork.

This might mean a lot of research and time for you at first, but really what you're doing is connecting yourself to the spirit of the earth. You don't want to rush this just for the sake of getting to whatever spell you want to work. The relationship you develop is a lifelong one and will serve you for years to come.

After your teas, do some research on the spices you have, the plants and flowers growing in your backyard or in pots. Next, you may want to look into how you can grow more herbs on your own. Eventually getting to the point where you don't have to buy a plant for a working.

The Power of the Root

"[W]e wouldn't ask why a rose that grew from the concrete for having damaged petals, in turn, we would all celebrate its tenacity, we would all love its will to reach the sun, well, we are the roses, this is the concrete, and these are my damaged petals, don't ask me why, thank god, and ask me how."

This Tupac Shakur quote speaks to the strength of the human spirit, but we also know that it speaks to the power hoodoo taps into: the power of roots.

We can use roses as an example of this; it's one many of us are already very familiar with in many cases. The roots of a rose pull energy from the earth to create a plant that is unique. Its smell is distinct, same with its petals.

We also know roses have thorns. It's as if in creating a rose, the Universe knew how popular it would be and built in a level of protection. Now, when we approach a rose, we do so with care.

These aspects of the rose aren't just things we made up, they contribute to the plant's power, contained in its spirit.

Rose has the power to attract, which is why they are so popular in love and attraction spells (and on Valentine's Day), specifically in drawing these things to the person doing the work, or the person who the work is being done for.

Without roots, however, the rose wouldn't exist. Roots survive, even with no sunlight, even under concrete. They do their work in the dark, away from what we can see and feel. They represent the work that happens in the spirit world, or unseen places.

If you're using a plant to keep negative energy away from your home, for example. You might be drawn to purchase or use mandrake root, a versatile part of the plant that it is said can be used in any working.

However, it's careless to buy a sachet of this root and just throw it in your working. Not only do you want to have your intent for your spell, but you also want to have an intent for why you're using the mandrake. You would also want to know whether or not this plant is right for your working based on its profile, and your relationship with the root.

Yes, your relationship.

Much like the spirit of your ancestors, you want to start and grow a relationship with the herbs, plants, and roots you're working with. You can start by getting still and introducing yourself to the spirit of the plant.

It's normal for this to seem odd at first, but this kind of respect is one hoodoo practitioners have built and cultivated for years.

The Power of Dirt

Just like you wouldn't throw any plant inside of a working without knowing what the plant is and why you're using it, you wouldn't collect and use dirt from just anywhere.

Especially not a graveyard.

As discussed in the section Working with Place, dirt from different locations can help with our magic. Aside from graveyards, these are commonly:
- Hospitals,
- Churches,
- Banks,
- Colleges or Universities,
- Courthouses,
- Casinos, and
- Rivers.

Folks definitely get creative when it comes to collecting dirt. Any place you come across has a spirit, and that spirit gets into the soil around and underneath. With the right process, you could technically collect dirt from anywhere, not just the ones listed above.

If you're in or around a major city, there's dirt from districts, like financial or fashion. You could potentially get dirt from a neighborhood, a beach, park, zoo, airport or bus terminal, community center, city hall, soccer or sports field, club, animal shelter, even an adult store.

There is dirt and dust used in hoodoo that doesn't come from a specific place but is tied to a circumstance or situation. One example is anvil dust, which is commonly substituted with magnetic dust in many spells. These two things are not the same.

Anvil dust is specifically collected from what is leftover in a blacksmith's shop, where hard work happens, and direct focus is necessary. Anvil dust is infused with that spirit.

Taking dirt from a place is taking some of the power for your own purposes, so before going out to collect dirt, you want to know why you're taking dirt and what you plan to do with it.

You also want to take with you something to leave in place of whatever you took. Coins are a common offering, as is rum or whisky. If you don't want to leave anything or disturb the roots, you can clean up any garbage left in the area and leave the space better than you found it.

Collecting graveyard dirt isn't for the novice practitioner, but if you do venture out, you want to ensure to collect at the right time. Take note of the cycle of the moon and time of day. As a general guide, collecting after midnight and in the early morning hours is best.

Another consideration is the exact location of the dirt collected, again, this is especially true when collecting graveyard dirt. Depending on your spell, you may want to collect dirt underneath a shadow, at the entrance or the four corners of the graveyard.

In this case, it is definitely safer to purchase from someone who is more experienced at collecting graveyard dirt, rather than collecting yourself. If you feel anything negative *at all*, leave the graveyard and do not collect any dirt.

Practitioners will also be sure to leave something in exchange for the dirt they collect.

Seeds, Roots, Barks, Leaves, and Herbs

A list of *some* common roots, barks and wood, leaves, and herbs that are commonly used in hoodoo.

Just because an item is listed here doesn't mean it will be available in your area. Note the roots you're interested in using, research what they are, and what they're used for before purchasing. In all cases, try to either find the plant yourself in nature, or purchase from a supplier that grows these plants for magical purposes, specifically.

I've tried to go with some of the more common natural elements, hopefully some that you can find easily or already have. You'll also want to research where a plant has a root and leaves that are used for different things, as in the case of Comfrey.

There are a few different ways these can be used in your magic.

As an offering to your ancestors or to deities. Many of the seeds, plants, roots, and herbs we use regularly were also used by our ancestors. Usually about half a teaspoon of herbs or seeds can be added onto a small plate and left on the altar once offered.

Burned as an incense. It's much easier to do this with some herbs and roots than others. Burning can heighten the vibration of a space and prepare an environment before a ritual or spell.

Added to your working. One of the easiest ways to use the power of seeds, roots, barks, leaves, and herbs is by adding them to a mojo bag, hoodoo lamp, or jar or bottle.

Dressing candles. In rituals or prior to meditation, some hoodoo spells require dressing of a candle, though you can also dress any candle that you're getting ready to use. If you've set an intention for the day, for example looking for a job, you can dress a candle with herbs that can help and let it burn while you're going about your day.

There are many other places that you can use. Dried leaves and herbs can be infused in water, for example, and in workings like hoodoo lamps and washes.

Keeping Note

When you start your practice, you'll soon discover it can be hard to keep track of what you have in your hoodoo pantry. Here's where keeping a magical record is useful. Some traditions would call this a 'book of shadows'.

There isn't really a hoodoo equivalent to a book of shadows, and it doesn't take long to figure out why. Keeping a diary of magick is something people who have the privilege of privacy do. This is why, in starting your hoodoo practice, you want to recognize that you can read a book like this or keep notes and not be in trouble should someone else discover what you're doing.

All this to say, if you're reading this, I'm pretty sure you can get a binder or some other notebook to write down how you're progressing in your practice.

Section out a few pages to keep track of what herbs you have in stock and if you'll need to resupply soon. Alternatively, you can keep a digital list of some sort. These can help with marking which items you need to get and when your stock is running low.

The point is to find a system that works. You don't want to go out to buy something only to get home and find you had it already.

Seeds

Caraway. Can be used to stop someone you love from straying away, also helpful for increasing mental powers, bringing in love, passion, and is said to be anti-theft. Offer on a love altar or add some seeds to a mojo bag.

Cardamom. For increasing the love in your life. Particularly useful to soothe your own heart if you've been hurt or in pain. Can help with your luck in love, and fidelity.

Celery. If placed under a pillow, can encourage prophetic dreams while sleeping, also increases psychic abilities and helps with concentration.

Chia. Not much is known about the magical properties of this seed, but if you have it in your pantry, some say it can be used to help stop gossip against you. Burn on a charcoal disc or use them to dress a candle for a ritual.

Coriander. Commonly used in love spells, for lust, can be added to wine in ground form (though be careful with this). Can be used to ease the pain of a breakup. Great for mojo bags or dressing candles ahead of love rituals.

Cumin. Can be used to keep evil away, cursing enemies, or increase fidelity in your relationships. Can also be used to prevent theft and for protection. Can be burned on a charcoal disc and used in workings.

Fennel. Use these if you are going through hard times and need some extra support. Good for healing spells. Also works in purification, strength, and protection. Tie in a satchel and hang in your home to protect your space from evil and unwanted energies.

Fenugreek. Commonly used for drawing in money. One way to use it is to keep some seeds in an open container on a kitchen counter or table, and add seeds to it over time. Can also be used in the home by adding seeds to floor washes.

Flax. Can help to ward off any harsh or angry energies. Used in spells for healing and drawing in money. Also called Linseed. Combine with a few coins and place on an altar for financial stability.

Mustard. Different types have different uses. White or yellow seeds are usually associated with faith, as the bible verse says. Yellow mustard seeds can be carried in a small bottle or amulet for faith and success.

Poppy. The highly potent drug opium is extracted from these seeds, which aligns with how it can be used in magic: to help with getting rest and feeling pleasure. Can also be used to confuse enemies or people who are in your way. Carry some seeds in a mojo bag or satchel.

Star Anise. Can increase your psychic ability and awareness. Carried to increase your luck and is said to be able to keep the evil eye away. Also used in money magic. Excellent for container spells or carried for luck, protection, and divination.

Roots

Adam & Eve Root. Available in two; one root is shaped like a large marble with a flat side and the other shaped like a large nail. Together, these roots can be used to attract love to you. If you're in a relationship, each partner can carry one of the roots to keep your union strong. These roots come from orchid plants, which are endangered in many parts of the United States.

Althaea. A protective healer. Use in your spells when you or someone else needs to ease a broken heart or any emotional discord. It is said to draw spirits to you that will help in whatever you need. Can be burned on a charcoal disc.

Angelica. The root of angels. This is often said to help women with feeling strong and protected. Add to a bath or personal skincare products, grow in a garden or balcony to protect your home.

Arrowroot. A multi-purpose plant that is often used in baking when converted to a powder. In magic, the powder is most often used for luck. Often used as a substitute for graveyard dust.

Marsh mallow. These look and feel nothing like marshmallows, rather very light pieces of grey paper. Used for psychic protection and to enhance your intuitive abilities. An ideal addition for mojo bags but can also be consumed as a tea. Also known as Althaea Officinalis.

Bat's Head. Also called Devil Pod, Vampire Root, Cat's Claw. This is an actual pod that appears to have eyes and a mouth. It looks a little scary but is considered a favorite among hoodoo workers. Used primarily for protection, but also has powers in granting wishes.

Dandelion. For strengthening psychic abilities. A plant that can aid in transformation and abundance. If you live in an area where there are many of these plants about, forage for your own instead of buying from a supplier. Be aware, dandelion leaves have slightly different uses than the root.

Calamus. To gain control over yourself, or to get the upper hand in situations where you need it. Also great for protection. Often used in work that has to do with domination; casting a spell or added to oils.

Comfrey. If you are planning to travel anytime soon, this root may be good to keep on hand. *Note that Comfrey leaves have different magical correspondences than the roots. Keep in the home or vehicle, any place where you want to protect things from being lost or stolen.

Culver's. A major purifier. Other names for this root are: Bowman's Root, Brinton Root, Culver's Physic, and Physic Root (yes, that's physic, and not psychic). If you need spiritual purification beyond what you can do on your own, an experienced practitioner may use this root.

Ginger. A root that is amazing for building confidence and going out into a brave new world. Next time you're in the market for ginger root, look for one that is shaped like a human--this is said to be a powerful magical tool. Use to add fire and speed to spells.

Ginseng. Used for various magical purposes, including protection, healing, love, sex, and general luck. Famously used to boost male virility. Burn to keep evil spirits away or carry to draw luck to you.

Gravel Root. For help in getting and maintaining a job. Additionally, it can be used to ease distress, so if you are having trouble at work, this root may be an ideal option. Best used when carried, especially while working.

Jezebel. Said to be used by sex workers to draw clients who are submissive and give good tips. Can be used equally well for cursing an enemy. Use in a money-drawing mojo bag or honey jar.

John the Conqueror. One of the most popular roots used in hoodoo. Used as an all-purpose root for confidence, strength, success, health, protection, and money. As your practice advances, you'll want to have this one handy. Used in any magick you need, to be carried or used in baths and washes.

Licorice. Generally used in spells about love and relationships. However, it is also often used for spells with the intent of gaining control. Can be carried to attract love or chewed to build confidence.

Mandrake. Another common all-purpose root used for wealth, health, love, and protection. As its name suggests, this root is shaped like a man and said to 'scream' when it is harvested. Keep in your home, on a mantel or altar, for protection. Place on top of money for financial abundance.

Valerian. For peace, harmony, love, and protection. May be helpful in situations where there's discord in a relationship. Also known as 'Vandal'. Can be burned, to hex, or burned with a yellow candle to clear a hex cast on you.

Verbena. An all-purpose. Noted to help with all of the usual life situations: money, love, protection, healing, and peace. Additionally, helpful with maintaining youth, helping with low vibrations and increasing creativity. Also known as 'Vervain'. Include in prosperity spells or carry with you when you need to be creative.

From Trees

Cedar. There's some disagreement on how this wood can help with your magic, but it's generally said to be protective and helpful with matters of the home. Available as wood chips, but branches are also used in incense. Can be burned for cleansing in the same way as sage and palo santo.

Frankincense. A massively powerful resin used in nearly all types of spells to boost their power. Usually burned on a charcoal disc to clear a space and to heighten vibration, so excellent to use ahead of rituals where you need extra power. Resin can also be offered to ancestors and deities on your altar.

Myrrh. Another powerful resin that can be used in the same way as Frankincense. Associated with Isis. Used for spiritual healing, to raise vibrations ahead of meditation or rituals. Excellent for blessing your space and magical tools and is a connector to the dead.

Palo Santo. This wood is sacred to Indigenous cultures in North America, and, as of 2019, was on the watch list for becoming endangered because of its popularity. It is generally burned and used for cleansing, but there are thousands of options for this, which is why I recommend steering clear of this wood for your use.

Pine Needles. An alternative to palo santo, if you're in the need of spiritual cleansing. In addition, said to attract prosperity. Pine trees survive in harsh conditions and are worth a try if you need some of that resilience in you, or your magic.

Leaves

Acacia. Used in spiritual practices and rites for thousands of years, in cultures around the world. A masculine all-purpose plant that can be used to clean and consecrate your magical tools. Burn, or use in washes.

Agrimony. A spell reverser. If you think or know someone has hexed you, this leaf can help and dissolve the things that can get in your way: depression, anger, sadness, fear, impatience, etc. Use in body washes and in oils.

Alfalfa. A leaf commonly used for money and financial abundance. In addition, it's also said to keep away poverty and hunger. Dispersing under a carpet in your home may help with attracting clients and customers for your at-home business,

Basil. All-purpose: love, cleansing, protection, attracting money, love, and abundance, must-have for any serious practitioner. Widely available in North America, considered sacred in some cultures. To use for blessing your home with prosperity and happiness, soak some dried herb in water for three days. Strain and sprinkle the water by your door.

Bay. Another all-purpose leaf that many practitioners across many different magical practices use regularly. Particularly effective at keeping evil away, specifically when dealing in hexes and curses. Write what you want on a leaf and burn it to draw in your desires. Excellent to purify the air (by burning) if someone sick has been in a room.

Catnip. Used for love, particularly by women who want to attract a specific man. Can also be useful in mojo bags for physical attractiveness and self-love. Can be carried to attract someone to you. Hang dried over your door to draw in luck and good spiritual energy.

Damiana. Another leaf used for love, and lust specifically. Also used to increase psychic ability and to help align the chakras. Helps build the energy of other magical herbs. Use as an offering on a love altar, or in sachets, honey jars, mojo bags, or candle working to draw love to you.

Eucalyptus. For healing and purification. Is also available as an essential oil, which can work in spells just as well as the leaf. Is said to help keep evil away and cleanse after being around lingering vibrations that you don't want around. Can be used for protection and for health when carried in a mojo bag or sachet.

Holly. Used for protection and drawing luck. The same leaf often associated with Christmas, so you'll find it hanging in practitioners' homes during Yule. Can draw protection for the home when burned with incense. Often used around Christmas time.

Lemon. Lemon leaves have similar magical properties to the fruit. Very effective for cleansing negative energy, especially from old or reused items. Leaves can be used for cleansing, either your body or home.

Marjoram. Can draw in wealth, protect, and dispel negativity. Is also considered good for the home. Good to carry around for money and for protection. Placed under pillows may bring you revealing dreams. Can be carried or placed in the home to draw love.

Mint. All types of mint are good for magic. Good for protection and healing. Peppermint specifically helps with feeling peace and keeping vibrations high. Place mint on your altar(s) to draw good energy and good spirits.

Mistletoe. Not considered a particularly strong leaf, but a good addition to boost your magic. A healer and protector. Can be hung in the home for protection or worn to prevent you from getting attention you don't want.

Oregano. An herb commonly used in food can also be protective and give your magick some added energy. Oregano leaves have been burned for centuries to keep negative energies away.

Passion Flower. Doesn't quite arouse passion but is useful in love spells and for building your social circle. Promotes sleep when placed under a pillow.

Patchouli. A masculine leaf that's useful for money and for love. Is also reported to be useful for breaking spells cast on you by someone else. Often used in spells, oils, and bags for love and for money. Can be placed in your wallet to draw money.

Pennyroyal. A protector against any negative vibrations, regardless of where they're coming from. Is useful to mend problems in the home, issues with family, or negative energy in the home. Can be worn or carried to keep negative vibrations away and help your business.

Rosemary. Another leaf used by many practitioners, particularly by women. Can both heal and protect. Also said to be useful in the home, particularly when hung dried over a window or door. Use to draw love or healing by creating a poppet of yourself and filling it with this herb.

Sage. Like Palo Santo, Sage is a leaf used for cleansing, blessing, and purification. Certain types of sage are specifically sacred to Native American cultures.

Thyme. A common spice in the kitchen, also used to draw money, and attract a positive reputation. It can be worn on the body or hung in the home to draw in protection and strength. If you tend to feel more mellow negative vibrations, like boredom, burn on a charcoal disc to change the energy and uplift.

Violet. Can be worn to keep a calm temperament and stay peaceful. May also help with drawing in love. Place leaves in a green mojo bag or sachet to heal physical and emotional wounds, and protect yourself when wounded.

Herbs

Allspice. Useful for boosting your luck in any situation. Can also help when it comes to finding treasure, or an added boost to any charms you already have. Berries that are available either dried, or as a powder. Burn for money and luck.

Asafetida. Said to help with repelling evil and can be used to bring difficulties to your enemies. Does not smell nice. Burn on charcoal and say your petition in the name of the devil to stop someone from bothering you.

Black Pepper. A common kitchen ingredient that can also be used to blast out and protect from negative energy. Can also keep positive energy away if used too much. Often used with other herbs in magick and rituals. Place around your wallet to dispel negative energy.

Buckeye Nut. Generally used for luck, particularly when chance is involved. Also used in drawing in money and with male virility. Carried in your pocket, this nut is said to draw luck and money.

Calendula. A flower used for psychic and spiritual powers, boosting your luck, and getting help when it comes to legal matters. Can be placed in a garland on your door to keep evil away. Useful in love working or as an offering on a love altar.

Chamomile. Widely used for healing, to diminish stress and clean an environment of any hexes, curses or lingering energy. Also useful for luck, bringing in money, and attracting love. Use in a bath for love.

Cinnamon. A fiery spice that can be burned for heightened spiritual abilities, for prosperity, and to raise your vibration. Beneficial for drawing in money and success. If you have cinnamon-burn it! It can draw money and love, purify, and aid your psychic abilities.

Cinquefoil. Can be useful when you're dealing with legal bodies, since it helps with finding your words. Five points represent love, money, power, health, and wisdom, and it's said this herb will impart those on anyone who wears it.

Cloves. Can be used for any magick related to fire (i.e. your willpower). Helps with money, love, and protection. Burning cloves as incense can work to attract money and raise vibrations.

Elder. Roots, leaves, berries, and flowers are major for protection, but are also poisonous, so be careful. Can be used to guard your home and your money-making endeavors. Can be worn for protection.

Garlic. Widely used to protect against all forms of evil, including vampires (energetic or otherwise). Healing and great for exorcising negative energies or entities. Hanging in the home won't protect against vampires but will boost your willpower and strengthen family bonds.

Hops. This beer flower is excellent in magick to help induce sleep and pleasant dreams. Also beneficial in healing and money magic. Use in dream pillows or to help with inducing restful sleep.

Hyssop. A mint mentioned in the bible (Psalm 51) for spiritual purification. Highly popular in magick for cleansing, particularly for washes and baths. Soak in water for a few days, strain and use the water to cleanse your magical tools and objects.

Jasmine. A flower that is good for attracting a soul mate and generally being open to love. Also useful for divination, drawing wealth, and charging crystals (quartz specifically).

Juniper Berry. Used for attracting love and increasing attraction and lust. Keeps things you don't want away and has the ability to attract good vibrations and health.

Lavender. A flower used to attract love, heal from depression. Promotes sleep and can help with purification. Highly popular as an essential oil. Burning the flowers and spreading ashes can help with love spells and rituals.

Mugwort. Often used to cleanse and purify tools used for divination, such as scrying mirrors. Can also help with fertility. Create a Mugwort 'tea' (or infusion) by mixing one teaspoon of the herb with one cup of boiling water and using this to clean your altar and magical tools.

Nettle. Nature's 'Return to Sender'. Return any spells or hexes cast on you, build your will, strengthen yourself and your ability to handle emergencies.

Nutmeg. Whole, helps with luck and winning at games where luck is needed. Can also be used to attract prosperity, protection, and helping to break a hex. Sprinkle on a green or white candle for use in prosperity spells, use in mojo bags, and satchels.

Red Pepper. Crushed or pods, have the same correspondence, cleansing and triggering a breakup of a relationship. Used for 'enemy' magic, to drive someone away or cause bad luck to someone else, often with other herbs like salt and black pepper.

Rose. The love flower. As a rose has its thorns, so does this flower's protective ability in magic. Can help with any matters of the heart, finding love, self-healing, and removing bad luck. Place roses on your love altar to honor Venus, goddess of love, beauty (and much more).

Skullcap. Used in money magic, also used to keep partners (usually the masculine energy) faithful in relationships. Can also be helpful in fostering peacefulness. Some of this herb in a lover's shoe is used to help keep them from being noticed by others.

Wormwood. Is said to be good for creating peace in war-like conditions. Also helpful in protection and assisting in receiving clairvoyant information. Can be carried or placed as protection from accidents, so in a satchel, bag, or car.

Yarrow. Popular in spells and workings for courage and self-confidence. Useful for healing and drawing love to anyone who wears it in a sachet. Rubbing over your eyes is said to help with clairvoyance.

Waters

Beware of applying waters, and the oils listed in the next section, on your skin or ingesting them. I do not recommend you put any of these on your skin or eat them, you have to know what is safe for you.

Florida Water. A widely popular in many magical practices, but hoodoo in particular. It is an all-purpose water that can be used across multiple purposes in your magic. Technically a cologne.
- Attract good spirits and repel negative ones.
- Cleanse your area before a working by using it in a spray.
- Add to your ancestor altar as an offering.
- Create a wipe for your altar and use for regular cleanings.
- Add to spiritual baths and scrubs. While Florida Water is considered safe for skin, you want to test this out first.

Kananga Water. Is a cologne used for spiritual cleansing and protection in the same way as Florida Water, though not as widely available.

Orange Water. Made with orange essential oil mixed in distilled water. Used topically, for those who are wishing to increase their luck or looking to get married. Offer on money and love altars. Use it as a wash in a bath or shower. Can also be added to your altar when doing rituals or prayers focused on love or fortune.

Peace Water. Like the name suggests, used to promote peace wherever it is used. Comes in an indigo blue color. Use on self-love or altars for the home. Sprinkle around your space after cleaning to encourage a peaceful environment.

Rose Water. Generally used on the body to attract love, also used in beautification rituals and spells. Can also be offered on love altars or to love goddesses. Add to baths and include it as an offering on your altar.

War Water. Used in witch wars and for hexing. Often contains an iron nail along with herbs and plants consistent with the purpose. *Definitely* not for drinking.

Willow Water. As a tree that grows near water and is often found in or around graveyards (usually in the South), willow water is good for healing, poured as an offering at gravesites. It's considered a natural remedy to physical ailments and can be offered on ancestor altars. Can also be presented as an offering to your herbs, plants, and roots.

Cleansing Oils

There are *many* different types of oils in the hoodoo practice. We're just going to list the cleansing oils here, but there is an oil for money and abundance, keeping your home peaceful, attracting love to you, hexing and blessing, breaking curses, and getting lucky.

To use the oils, you can anoint yourself, anoint any special paperwork you're using for a working or just in your life. You can anoint your altar or tools used on your altar, such as statues of deities. You can also use oils to bless your personal items, such as a wallet.

For this section of the book, we'll focus on just the oils for cleansing. As we'll cover in future chapters, cleansing and protection are very important when you're working with spirit.

Cut & Clear. An oil you'll find at almost any hoodoo shop. For cutting and clearing anything out of your life, such as habits, exes, and attachments. Anoint yourself, use in personal care products, wear on your body like a perfume.

Dragon's Blood. Considered a powerful all-purpose oil. Is red in color from Dragon's Blood, a deeply red-colored resin. Add some drops to your cleaning products or use to anoint your tools and altar.

Hindu Grass. An oil for cutting out things from your life. This could be a relationship or a pattern of thinking or behavior, ties to past events. An oil you can use on yourself, anointing and wearing.

Blessing. There's Blessing oil, *and* House Blessing oil. The first type is generally used for yourself, the second strictly for your home. These oils cleanse and are said to help bring favor from deities. Depending on the type of oil, you can use it on yourself or for your home. You could also offer this oil to your ancestors or deities you're working with by leaving some drops on a plate or leaving an open jar on your altar.

Psychic Cleansing. If you need a psychic cleansing of old energies weighing you down or getting in your way, try a psychic cleansing oil. Anoint yourself before meditating or offer some of the oil on a self-love altar.

Purification. A blaster of any blocks or energies that remain in your way. Not as available as the other oils, but an excellent option if you're just getting out of a bad relationship or attachment. Burn this oil on a charcoal disc or add it to a self-healing mojo bag.

Part II: Spells, Tricks, and Rituals

Now that you have some basic information about the basics of hoodoo, in this section of the book we'll be going over some specific spells, tricks, and rituals you can incorporate into your practice.

'Tricks' here are not about doing something to your friends to have a laugh. A 'trick' in hoodoo is another way to say 'spell'. The terminology you'll often hear is 'laying down a trick', 'fixing tricks', or 'laying down'.

This meaning is on purpose. If you think of the origins of hoodoo, using these terms sound more or less inconspicuous. Telling someone you're going to 'lay down' doesn't sound odd to most of us. But using this code was very important to earlier practitioners to avoid the punishment of being accused of engaging in hoodoo.

Preparing to Work with Roots

Buying roots from a supplier you trust is a convenient way to get what you're looking for without going outside and foraging or searching for what you need in your environment. However, every hoodoo practitioner I know would rather go out and forage.

Most of us are used to living around plants every day but we don't pay much attention to them aside from watering and watching out for bugs. A good practice to start now (if you're not doing it already) is to go outside and take note of what's growing in your neighborhood and region.

No matter what you're going through, there's probably a plant that grows in abundance in your backyard that can help. In this section, we'll cover what you'll need to successfully forage for roots.

Root Reverence

Before you head out, you will have to do some research on what's available in your neighborhood and local wooded areas.

It's best to go out with an intent, for example, if you know you want to find wild strawberries for a working, you'll know what it looks like and where it's most likely to grow. On the other hand, you can search around and take photos of what you find, whatever looks interesting, and then do your research at home.

Even if you're planning to purchase from a local retailer, you want to know if what they're selling is available to you locally. Not only could this potentially save you money, but you'll also know if what you're buying is endangered.

Hoodoo is where you get to really put your hands into the work. The plants you touch will have their own spirit, as we've discussed, and in preparing to work with plants, you want to honor these spirits.

When you're foraging, you are taking a plant from its natural habitat for your own purpose. This isn't wrong, the plants we use are given to us by mother nature for our use (everything in nature is created for the use of everything else), so foraging requires some respect and care.

Introduce yourself to the spirit of the plants and tell them what your intent is. While foraging, you want to stay open to communication from the plants you're touching. You do not have to speak out loud, you can do this all in your mind. Express gratitude for mother earth, to nature, for providing the materials we use to survive, and what you're taking for your working.

This reverence is part of the practice.

The Practice

The relationship you build with the roots, and all of the tools and materials you use for your magick is somewhat similar to the relationship you have with your ancestors. With all of the herbs you have in your home, or any plant you purchase, it does not work to bring it home and start casting a spell with it right away.

Once you have some privacy, it's time to consecrate the herbs and start building your connection.

Start by putting some of the roots in your palm and holding them. Take a moment to smell and get acquainted. saying a prayer of thanks. You can open your prayer by saying something like: "Mother Goddess, I come to you now in respect," and then continue with acknowledging the herb or seed you're holding.

Say that you are welcoming their spirit into your space. At some point, you can recite Psalm 23 over the roots in your palm (you'll probably want to have this one memorized).

Your prayer can include a reference to what work you intend to do with the root and what your highest intentions are. Speak slowly and take note of how you feel. Create in yourself a feeling of gratitude; you may be already feeling this as you pray.

Everything you have is there to help you, no matter what change you want to make in your life. Share your gratitude with the spirits you speak to; you're going to get what you want, and the spirits are ready and willing to help.

Bless your roots after your prayers. Breathe deeply and open yourself up to an experience of your own power. If you need some help with this, think of your own divine self. Choose to identify with the part of yourself that has no problems, breathe and connect with the part of you that knows all of the answers to your problems.

Then, as you're standing in your power, say: *I bless the spirit of [name the item]*. Continue to offer your thanks, acknowledge the specifics of *that* spirit.

For example, if you're connecting with the spirit of Fennel Seeds, acknowledge their strength, specifically through hard times, how they can heal and protect.

You may want to share how you can learn from this spirit, and how in your relationship you intend to keep your ears and heart open to their guidance. In case you're wondering, yes, Fennel Seed was very important to me in my own hard times.

In terms of offerings, you may see other practitioners blowing smoke on the roots or spilling alcohol like whiskey. These are offerings.

If you don't have whiskey or a cigar/cigarette, your words of praise, songs, or coins will suffice. Present these things the same way you would to your ancestors.

You want to regularly speak to and pray over your roots and make offerings in whatever form of your choosing.

You'll want to repeat this process (or something like it, with your modifications) over everything that has a spirit and that you intend to use for your working. This includes candles, crystals, waters, and oils.

Time and Space

A root burrowed deep into the ground is an admirable thing. Of course, for most plants we never see it happening. The only way to know for sure that a root exists is by what we do see.

It's work that is done and happens by the force of nature alone, and the deeper and thicker the roots, the more time it has taken for growth to happen.

Roots grow and do their thing with little human intervention. And even when humans do intervene, it's seldom necessary.

This is one of the reasons time is important. A plant needs to be given enough time to grow before it's pulled from the earth. Once it's been harvested, the growth process stops.

Yes, nature is abundant and regenerative, but that is exactly what it is that we deeply respect and are grateful for.

There are many considerations that will dictate when and where you forage: season, time of year, time of day, moon cycle, and location are a few.

Season

Not every plant can be picked in every season. Berries are probably the best way to demonstrate this. You can't pick a berry that isn't ripe. Depending on the berry, this could be Fall, as in with Elderberries. Or summer, as with cherries.

However, some plants and seeds can be foraged year-round, depending on where you live, like Acorns for example.

Time of Day

Another factor to consider when harvesting is the time of day you're out and picking plants for their roots.

Some plants would be best picked early in the morning, while dew is still on the leaves. Others, it would be better to pick at night. The only way to know for sure is to know what you're picking.

Moon Cycle

To get the highest magical potency from the roots, you'll also want to consider what cycle the moon is in.

If you're not familiar with how to do this, an online search for 'moon cycle' will show you where the moon is for the time of month. With most calendars you can also see when the moon will be full or new, which can help you plan your foraging day.

Time of Year

Gardening by the Moon says that the moon also determines the best times of year to plant, weed, prune, and harvest plants.

When the moon is in Aries, Leo, Sagittarius, Gemini, or Aquarius, it's considered the best time to harvest. For this information, you could buy an almanac, but these dates are also widely available online.

You may be able to find a calendar that tells you what phase the moon is in (i.e. waning crescent, new, waxing, full), and what sign it's in, but if not, you will have to look this information up separately.

Location

Unless you have a backyard where you can grow plants already, you'll most likely be out at a park or forested area nearby.

You could go out and take what you need in the moment, however many experts recommend watching the plant you're planning to harvest over some time, at least a month.

This might be more difficult if you're foraging at a local wooded area or park, but it's really not much more than going for a walk and checking in on your chosen plant.

If you're looking to do a spell quickly this might seem like an unnecessary wait, but as a beginner, you want to take your time with hoodoo, and foraging especially. Not having the right energy in the roots you find will impact your magic.

There are many reasons a spell may not work in the way you expected or intended, foraging with the wrong energy or at the wrong time could be the reason this happens, but you want to mitigate this as much as possible.

The only way to do that is to build a relationship with the plants you need before finding them in nature. Roots you take time to cultivate a relationship with will be more powerful as a part of your magic.

Equipment and Tools

When finding roots, you want to get as much of the root as possible. There will be small pieces left behind, but if you're harvesting for roots, you will be collecting whole plants.

You may not use the whole root in your working, so this way you can use what you need for your work, and replant what you don't use, either in your backyard or a pot in your home.

Does this mean you'll potentially have a house full of plants? Hopefully.

The tools you'll need to collect roots are simple: **gloves (the gardening type)** and something to dig the roots out with. This can be a type of **gardening knife called a 'Hori Hori'**, but you can also use a **garden fork**. To snip herbs or flowers, you'll need **scissors** to make a clean cut of the stem.

When it comes to carrying and storing what you forage, you'll want to have a bag handy just for what you collect. You may also want to have string on hand if you plan to hang dried herbs.

In the next section, we're covering some basic techniques for making extractions from the herbs and plants you forage or have on hand. You certainly do not have to know how to extract from plants, but it can be helpful if you want to conserve the essence of some of the herbs you have.

For extraction, you'll need some of the common tools most hoodoo practitioners have:

1. A mortar and pestle.
2. Alcohol (a high-quality rum can be used for extraction, and for offerings to your ancestors and to your roots and herbs).
3. Empty bottles. Try to get ones that are easy for you to clean. Some extracts may be sensitive to light. In this case, darkly colored bottles are recommended.
4. Something to filter with, like a sieve or some cheesecloth.

Often other common kitchen tools are used in extraction, like a small kitchen fan used to circulate air. You may also use pots and pans and a stove to bring substances to a boil.

Getting some **disposable gloves** is also a good idea, especially if you are dealing with more volatile substances or hoodoo powders. You probably already have a mask you can use to prevent yourself from breathing in any fumes, but these are also good to keep on hand.

Gathering and Drying Herbs

Another common practice among many practitioners is drying herbs that have been gathered, usually in a bunch hanging by a window or door, but there are a few methods to drying, such as sun drying or using a microwave-yes, microwave drying is possible!

You can hang any herb with a stem to dry. such as marjoram, basil, and mint. So, when gathering your herbs, make sure to give yourself lots of stem, especially if you're going to use the hang-drying method described below.

Herbs need to be completely dried before being stored, especially if you're planning to use jars or containers. If not, you'll be trapping your herbs in with water, which is great if for creating mold (though fungi have been used in magic, so there's probably some use for mold as well).

After gathering your herbs, carefully wash them and remove any debris or dead material, if you see it. Adding water will, of course, mean your drying time will be longer, so if you don't see anything to wash off, feel free to skip this step.

Once your herbs are clean, gather them in a bunch by the stems. It should look like you have a small bouquet of herbs. Use string or a rubber band to secure the bunch. Once tied together, they can be hung from your roof or a drying rack. A tea towel or j-cloth underneath the herbs will catch any falling drops.

While it looks pretty, hanging your herbs to dry may not be the most effective, since these herbs will often collect dust and stuff floating in the air. Left too long, and you'll soon start to see dried leaves and flowers falling onto the ground.

To prevent this, you can secure the bunched herbs within a paper bag. Though this is optional. Many herbs can be magical just hanging to dry. It all depends on your intent.

With a few candles and some herbs hanging around, your space can really start to look and feel like a magical home.

If you'd prefer not to hang dry, you can use the sun or other heat sources. For sun drying, you'll need to put your clean herbs on a screen or other porous surfaces. Most people will use the screen from a door. This is to give the moisture already in the plant somewhere to go and to make it easier for air to circulate.

You'll also want to put something underneath where your herbs are sitting, again to catch water. As the name suggests, you'll set leaves on the screen and leave them in the sun until they're dry.

Keep in mind: this is sun drying, not moon. If you leave herbs out for a day and they aren't dry, you'll have to take them inside overnight. This way you keep the morning dew from slowing the process down.

The last alternative is microwave drying. You want to be careful with this method because left in the microwave for too long, and you can burn the herbs or worse, start a fire. This is also why it's important to remove any excess moisture from your leaves first.

Once the herbs are as dry as you can make them, place them in the microwave in a single layer, in between two sheets of paper towel. Set the microwave for a minute on high and check the leaves. Continue heating the leaves for 30 seconds at a time, checking each time.[1]

Storage

Your dried leaves can then be stored in an airtight container, in a cool, dry space away from direct sunlight and away from heat.

Air is not a friend to your dried herbs, so however you choose to store, make sure that the container is airtight. Humidity in the air can undo the work you put into drying your herbs.

Regarding a 'cool, dark place', most of the time a fridge is a fine spot, but if that's not available, any spot that is out of the sunlight will do.

---

[1]Herb Gardening: Harvesting, Drying and Storing Herbs. (2021). Herb Gardening: Harvesting, Drying and Storing Herbs. https://web.extension.illinois.edu/herbs/tips.cfm#:~:text=With%20proper%20storage%2C%20most%20herbs,the%20sides%20of%20the%20bags.

Last, take note of the herbs you dried, which method you used, and the date you put the herbs into storage. This is good practice for your kitchen, so you might have a place to note these details down already.

Dried herbs don't necessarily expire, but as with most foods, they do have a 'best before' date. Generally, the time frame for dried herbs is two years, sometimes three. However, this doesn't mean that you can't use the herbs after that date.

Mojo Bags

A mojo bag is a very popular working in hoodoo. It is also one of the first things you want to create as you start your practice.

The hoodoo definition of mojo is spirit.

We talked about containment in a previous section. This is a concept specific to the Yoruba tradition, out of western Africa.

A mojo bag is about concentrating the energy of spirit in work towards whatever your intent.

You generally can't go wrong when creating one of these for your personal use. You can find many, many spells for mojo bags online or in hoodoo books. It makes a great first spell for beginners because you are encouraged to get creative.

One practitioner I know used a name necklace that broke in such a way that their name was split almost in half. She wasn't interested in getting the piece fixed, but she also didn't care to throw it away because it meant something to her. The broken necklace made a perfect addition to her self-love mojo bag. Her intent in creating the bag was to heal a broken spirit.

Generally, the purpose of these bags is to draw love, money, success, or protection to you. You can use it while you're working to create a larger change in your life.

Let's say, for example, that you want to draw in real romantic love. Not just a new boyfriend or girlfriend (or boyfriends or girlfriends), but a true shift in your outlook on love.

You know, however, that this will require a change in your mindset and you're not sure about what this will look or feel like.

With a mojo bag, you can get help making this deeper shift so that when your love spell works, you don't block the love you deserve.

The rules for a mojo bag are simple:
1. No one but you is to touch, see, or use your mojo bag for any reason. We're all used to keeping things in secret, that applies here as well.
2. You can either keep it on you all the time, or every day over a period, like a week or lunar cycle, depending on what you're using it for.

Making a Mojo Bag

Traditionally, mojo bags are made out of flannel. Most people think of the plaid type of shirts when they hear that name, but flannel is a yarn or wool material, and is not specific to a pattern. You can get flannel cloth in any color you want. Which is good when it comes to working hoodoo.

In addition to carefully choosing the color, you want to get flannel in a material that feels good on your skin. This is especially true if you plan to wear your bag close to you over a period of months or weeks.

It might seem excessive to buy a whole yard of flannel online, just to create a relatively small item. Another option may be searching through your closet to see if you have any flannel that will work or checking with anyone who may want to donate some fabric to you.

However, most flannel is available cheaply priced, and if you enjoy making a mojo bag, with enough fabric you can make bags for your friends and family.

You want to create a mojo bag with intention, in the same way that you would create your altar.

You can also imagine that the items that go inside can include things you would put on an altar; curios (small items like figurines and symbols), herbs, oils (usually in small glass jars or container), crystals and energy stones, dried plants, petitions to spirit, hair or fingernails, coins and dollar bills, jewelry, and, of course, roots.

There are two different ways you can make one of these bags for yourself, depending on how comfortable you are with a needle and thread. For the mojo bags below, you will need your flannel and string, again, in a color that *speaks* to you and your working. However, the simple and effective choice in many cases may be to go with your favorites.

Before creating your mojo bag, you'll want to do a good cleanse and prayer over *everything* you'll be using to create and make your bag.

One thing I have not included in the ingredient lists below is *you*. In each mojo bag you create for yourself, you must include inside something that has your DNA, your energetic signature. This can be as simple as the breath.

After all of the ingredients, adding your breath can be saying your intention at the mouth of the bag or over the ingredients inside. You want your breath to come into contact with the ingredients you've put inside.

Other than your breath, you can include hair, toenails, fingernails, spit, blood; anything that comes from your body. Most practitioners would recommend adding some substance of yours, such as your toenails, and your breath.

You want to keep your mojo bag as close as possible to your body for at least a week.

The advantage of the sewing option is the ability to create a satchel that can hold more than the non-sewing option.

The Sewing Option

1. Cut a piece of flannel cloth, 4 inches wide by 12 inches long.
2. Fold the flannel in half on the "wrong" side so the bag is 4 inches wide by 6 inches long.
3. Sew inside about a quarter inch along the long edges, leaving the top open.
4. Flip inside out, and now you have a little bag.

5. Pray over and bless each item before putting it inside. As you fill your bag, you will start to feel the energy building.
6. Tie string around the closure or create a simple drawstring.

The Non-Sewing Option

This type of mojo bag is commonly called a 'flaming comet' because once tied closed, it looks like a comet.

You'll want to cut your flannel in the shape of a square; 5in. x 5in. is sufficient. The idea is to put all of your materials in the middle and then gather the ends and secure the string around, so everything is contained tightly inside.

Ingredient Lists

Now that you know how to make a basic mojo bag (you can, of course, get more elaborate if you have more advanced sewing skills), here are a few basic recipes for common workings. All of these are designed to be interchangeable; some of the items may be a little difficult to get, but if there's one you want to make, get creative and substitute anything you don't have for items you *do* have, or can get easily.

Each recipe has a few color options for your flannel. You'll also find most recipes include: a small symbolic object, a natural element (such as a root or dried herb), one or two crystals.

The reason I am not providing you with a specific recipe is because there is no way for me to know what speaks to you. Hopefully, upon reading the lists below, you'll have the materials you need to create your own mojo bag already. If not, at least the options will inspire you.

However, you need to know how the different elements you're using work together and how these elements will aid in your working. For example, let's say you have no problem attracting money, but you're creating a mojo bag to help with keeping money and growing your investments. You may not want to include a citrine stone in your mojo bag, since this stone is more about manifesting wealth.

Do not include anything in your mojo bag that you don't connect with, or that doesn't mean anything to you.

Speaking of energy, I would recommend not creating any of these mojo bags if you're in an agitated emotional state. This is especially true if you're creating a bag for money, inner peace, healing, or luck. You can purchase the most expensive materials from people who grow and create items for magick specifically, but your energy will change everything if you're not careful.

Another name for a mojo bag is a 'hand'. An apt name, since to make these bags, you use your hands. If your energy is off in any way, that is going to transfer through your body, through your hands, and go into the bag you're creating.

Before you begin praying and cleansing, get as calm as possible. If you can't get calm, choose another date or time to create the bag. Create a feeling of excitement. As you create your bag, keep in mind that you're getting everything you want, and the specific circumstances that led you to create this mojo bag! Think and agree with yourself that every item you're using to create your bag will *work for you*.

A few elements listed below are universal, meaning you can use them for any of the bags listed. Instead of going for a generic green, for example, choose a shade that aligns with your intent. For an inner peace or inner healing mojo bag you might go with a sage green, while for money you could use an emerald green.

In addition, often you'll find crystals that are molded into different shapes, for example, a rose quartz in the shape of a heart or a jade stone in the shape of a frog. These objects can do double or triple duty in your mojo bag, if used with intention.

I should note that while white is a universal shade for magic, a mojo bag is created to be carried with you all the time, which would mean it may show dirt easily. Consider using white for the items you place inside of your bag. Otherwise, be prepared to clean your bag constantly.

For Inner Peace

Flannel Color Options: Green, Blue, Yellow, Pink, Black.
Charm Options: Peace symbol, peace hand, dove, feather, or a charm with the word 'peace' engraved.
Crystal Options: Selenite, moonstone, pink opal, opalite, blue lace agate, rose quartz, alone or combined with amethyst, petrified wood, scolecite.
Herb and Nature Options: Chamomile, Lavender, skullcap, vervain, or verbena.
Place Options: Dirt from a church. Small seashells from a beach, smooth stones, like those found in a park or a wooded area.

For Money

Flannel Color Options: Green, purple, red.
Charm Options: Currency symbols, like a dollar sign, tree, acorn, infinity symbol, a cup (to represent your cup being full), sun and/or stars.
Crystal Options: Pyrite, citrine, red garnet, green aventurine and/or jade, clear quartz, tiger's eye, malachite, amazonite, tree + moss agate (combined), lapis lazuli.
Object Options: Dollar wrapped in white or green or gold thread, coins, specifically if you can find coins minted.

Herb and Nature Options: Bay leaf, alfalfa, bee pollen, catnip, star anise, sugar, peppermint, basil leaf, patchouli leaf.
Place Options: Dirt from a bank.
Roots: Licorice Root, Mandrake Root.

For the charm, you may want to include a trinket that represents anything you desire, for example, a small yacht, a model car, a home, even a beach umbrella. You may also want to use anything that symbolizes abundance or wealth in your culture. Salmon, for example (Native American).

For Luck

Flannel Color Options: Green, orange, red.
Charm Options: Four-leaf clover, elephant, horseshoe, a key, dice, ladybugs, a number 7, evil eye, sun and/or stars.
Crystal Options: Smoky or clear quartz, labradorite, amethyst, carnelian, tiger's eye.
Object Options: A penny or coin you've found.
Herb and Nature Options: Star anise, buckeye nuts.
Place Options: Dirt from a casino.
Roots: High John the Conqueror.

For Love

Flannel Color Options: Pink, red, green.
Charm Options: Heart, rose, cupid, swans, doves, (any animal that is said to mate for life), a Claddagh ring, ankh.

Crystal Options: Rose quartz, aventurine, malachite, moonstone, lapis lazuli, garnet, amazonite, citrine, rhodonite, hibiscus flower.

Object Options: An object from a wedding you've attended. An image of the person who is your love interest*.

Herb and Nature Options: Cardamom, fennel seeds, rosemary, rose petals, lavender petals, oregano, patchouli, yarrow, thyme, basil.

Place Options: Dirt from a church.

Roots: Mandrake.

The charm idea from the money mojo recipe above applies here as well. Any object that means love to you will work in your mojo bag. This could be a small music note, if you love music, a little spoon, a book, or teddy bear.

About Love Spells in General

Here's where I address the little * on the object option above. Magic for love is a controversial topic.

Some practitioners refuse to do love spells for themselves, or for anyone else. They say that when it comes to love, they do not want to mess with another person's free will. They want to know that the person who is in love with them is making their own choice and is not manipulated by any outside forces. I am inclined to agree.

Often, when someone wants a love spell done on a person who is refusing to be with them, there are deeper self-love issues involved. Specifically, a lack of self-love.

Balance is *essential* when it comes to love spells. If you or a person who wants work done is 'stuck' on someone else for whatever reason, that points to an imbalance.

When it comes to love, what 'balance' means is often skewed. We can confuse getting what we want to mean balance, when this universal law has nothing to do with our desires. Often the best choice is to heal and move forward.

For Self-Love and Inner Healing

Flannel Color Options: Green, black.
Charm Options: Sun, yin-yang, lotus, cosmogram, rod of Asclepius (a snake coiled around a rod). Anything with silver.
Crystal Options: Amethyst, prehnite, ocean jasper, sunstone, pink opal, rhodochrosite.
Object Options: An image of yourself or some other object that represents you.
Herb and Nature Options: Yarrow, peppermint, rosemary, sage, chamomile, rose, lemon balm, honey, hibiscus, cinnamon, cardamom.
Place Options: (See above)

For Health and Physical Healing

Flannel Color Options: Green, red, orange, yellow, blue.

Charm Options: Rod of Asclepius (a snake coiled around a rod), a heart, mini-workout equipment, like a running shoe or dumbbell, a woman's or man's body.

Crystal Options: Red jasper, fuchsite, amazonite, seraphinite A+, golden healer quartz, fire agate.

Object Options: Your picture or a picture of the person you're creating this bag for. A petition for healing a specific issue.

Herb and Nature Options: Caraway, chia seeds, cinquefoil, coriander, ginger, ginseng, heal all, high john the conqueror, juniper berry, magnolia flowers, mandrake, pumpkin seed, rosemary, sage, sassafras, tansy, thyme.

Place Options: Dirt from a hospital or place of physical fitness.

For Success in Career

Flannel Color Options: Green, gold, purple, orange, brown, red.

Charm Options: A star (gold, specifically), small electronic devices, like a phone or computer, currency signs, a pen (to signify signing contracts), an award or trophy.

Crystal Options: Pyrite, citrine, fluorite, green aventurine, lapis lazuli, amazonite, carnelian, tiger's eye.

Object Options: A petition with the type of success you're looking for. Make it long-term, if this is a mojo bag you want to keep for a while.

Herb and Nature Options: Basil, bay leaf, bergamot, chamomile, cinnamon, clover, frankincense (a resin), ginger, high john the conqueror, hollyhock, honeysuckle, lo john the conqueror, lucky hand root, mustard seed, pecan, pennyroyal.

Place Options: Dirt from a bank or financial center in a city.

For Protection

Flannel Color Options: Black, blue, red, purple.

Charm Options: The eye of Horus, pentagram, arrow, scarab beetle, bear (or any animal that speaks 'protection' to you), dragon. The evil eye is a very common charm for protection.

Crystal Options: Black tourmaline, shungite, clear Lemurian crystal, quartz (clear or smoky), pyrite, turquoise, pink tourmaline.

Object Options: An image of yourself.

Herb and Nature Options: Acorn, African violet, angelica, asafoetida, basil, bay leaf, betel nut, black pepper, black pepper, calendula flower, chrysanthemum, cloves, dill, elderberry, eucalyptus, garlic, ginger, high john the conqueror, lavender, mandrake, marjoram, marshmallow root, peony, petitgrain, rice, salt (all types, but different colors have different energies. Pink salt, for example, for a more loving protective energy), vervain.

Place Options: Dirt from a bank or try dirt from a gated community.

Q: How do I put oil and dirt in my mojo bag without making a mess?

The mess isn't such a bad thing. Mojo bags aren't made with the position that the ingredients will be used again, so feel free to let all of the elements and energies mix about.

If you do want to keep some ingredients contained, you can reuse or find very small containers, especially the kind with a cork or porous closure.

A local dollar store is a great place for these, but any supply or arts and crafts shops usually have them.

Q: Can I create a mixed mojo bag? For example, luck and money?

It might be better to approach creating your mojo bag from the perspective of what you want and what you need. So instead of creating a 'luck and money' mojo bag, create a money mojo bag that includes elements that will bring you luck, for example, a penny or coin you found, an elephant, or clear quartz.

One combination you may want to consider making for yourself is a self-love mojo bag, as I mentioned above.

There are thousands of stones and crystals out there with different correspondences. A stone-like pink and green tourmaline, for example, is said to help with overcoming problems with father figures. If you're harboring pain from childhood related to your father, you might want to consider a stone like this for an inner healing mojo bag.

This said, I must caution you to not get too worried if you can't find a very specific stone for what you need.

Just like the thousands of crystals available from every corner of the world, there are countless ways you can combine elements to make a mojo bag that is just right for you. Don't distract yourself and waste energy looking for something you don't really need.

The herbs and items you have right now can contribute to a very powerful mojo bag because it will speak to *you* in a way that is unique to your energy.

Magic Candles

As you begin your hoodoo work, you'll quickly discover the importance of candles. When it comes to depicting magick this is one of the things Hollywood gets right.

Hoodoo candles aren't just the pretty pillars you can get at a dollar store or local home decor store, though the candles you can buy at these spots can work just as well as candles made with magical intention.

Your first hoodoo candle will probably be called a 7-day candle. These are available in a tall, glass cylinder, and as their name suggests, are built to last seven days. They are about 8 inches high and just over 2 inches in diameter.

You may have seen religious 7-day candles before. These are the ones with religious figures depicted on them, like Mother Mary, and may have a prayer printed on the back.

You can get plain candles, or ones in various colors. A 7-day candle may have seven different colors or two. These different colors can help you with blessing your candle, and with doing spells that require you to do a working every day for a week.

Some spells require you to bless a candle halfway up and halfway down. Two-colored 7-day candles show you easily where the halfway mark is.

One kind of candle you can purchase can have multiple colors, sometimes two, but you can find candles with up to seven colors in a column, as if each color is stacked one on another.

Another type of candle that is easier to use for spells that are not designed to last over a week, are smaller, thinner pillars in different colors. You could make these candles stand on something by melting the wax at the bottom and sticking the candle down on whatever you're working on.

Using a Lamp

In addition to candles, part of your practice can include the use of hoodoo lamps. If you have a traditional lamp at home, consider yourself lucky. You can use these lamps in your hoodoo.

More often, you'll find the kind of lamp that is created using a mason jar or other glass-type of container. Most of your magical items and ingredients will go inside of the jar with your oil. Your floating wick would then go on top of the oil and you can light it to activate your lamp.

What you're creating will look different from anything you may have seen in the past. Even in the hoodoo tradition, there aren't many people who create lamps. That said, it is not complicated.

At the end of your working, you'll most likely have your lamp sitting on a plate with different curios and items floating inside of the glass, with your flame or wick burning on top. On the plate, you may have more curios or items with the purpose of bolstering your working.

Generally, these floating wicks can last up to 24 hours, but you never want to leave an open flame by itself.

Foot Track Magick

We've covered how important hands are in hoodoo. Your hand has the power to create life, specifically the life you want to live by your work.

In hoodoo, the feet are arguably just as significant as hands, though in different ways. You'll see this in foot track magick, which is often used as a way to control or cause strife in another person's life.

If you think of what the foot means, literally and metaphorically, you'll see how many opportunities there are with a bit of hoodoo.

There's the path you walk in real life, and then the one you walk every day. You can 'step over' someone to get ahead in life, walk around obstacles in your way, or with someone else in a love relationship. You can walk out of someone's life, walk a mile in someone else's shoes, walk the straight and narrow, or walk right into something (usually a joke at your expense). I could go on, but you get the point.

Cursing and Hexing

One of the most popular ways foot track magick is used is to hex or curse someone else. The reason why this can be so effective is (if you'll allow me another metaphor) people often do not watch where they're going. Because of this, it can also be very easy to hex someone with foot track magick.

Most of the time, all you need to do is lay the trick down on a place where you know your target will walk, often by their front door. Once the person steps over or walks through the trick, the magick takes effect. In other words, they step in 'it'.

In life, where you're going determines what you do every day and how you live. Foot track magick, then, has the ability to affect others in some serious ways.

Most of these spells have the power to stop someone in their tracks and force them off of their life path. These spells usually work to confuse, deter, and distract the subject of the working.

These spells can also sometimes cause a wide range of physical symptoms.

Because this is dealing with negative spirits, who must be invited in for the work, often when someone wants to work a curse on someone else (and any type of curse, not just the foot track kind) a professional is hired. The bottom line is, doing something to impact someone else will return to you in some way.

Protection and Love

You can also work foot magick on yourself. For example, putting violet leaves in your shoes is said to attract love to you. Protection spells can also be cast on your shoes, or you can use knot magick on your shoelaces (though knot magick isn't considered hoodoo, specifically).

When it comes to love, foot track magick is often used to keep a lover in line. As mentioned in the herbs section, skullcap can be placed in your lover's shoe to help with keeping them faithful.

Spiritual Cleansing

When we go outside or interact with people, we are constantly in touch with energy: other people's or the energy of an environment.

You've probably felt this when you walked into a room where there was a tense argument or come across someone you did not have a good feeling about.

There are more subtle ways energy affects us that can go unnoticed. Groups of people can have a certain energy that can affect you. This is one of the reasons awareness is so important.

And the effect energy can have on your aura is one of the reasons cleansing is so important.

You can carry stones or a mojo bag for protection but doing this alone will put a lot of stress on your mojo bag. Your own cleansing will assist greatly with staying centered and protected.

There are also more serious cases that warrant cleansing, but I will caution you to not get too wrapped up in the possibility that you've attracted negative entities. There are some common emotional states, however, that you need to be aware of so you know what's possible, and why cleansing is so important.

Feeling lonely, depressed, or sad for prolonged periods of time can lead to being visited by energies and entities that feed off of this type of energy.

The unfortunate thing here is that often a person who is depressed does not know if they're being visited by an entity. The thoughts they have every day seem like their own thoughts, not things they are being told by an entity.

Even a passing comment by a stranger or an awkward encounter can affect your energy. The encounter itself wouldn't necessarily leave you open to spiritual attack, it's how your energy is affected afterward.

Before getting into the details of cleansing rituals, one thing you need to know is: cleansing and protection go hand in hand when it comes to magick. After every cleansing ritual you do, always protect.

For these rituals, you can use many Psalms, but a few I'll call out are Psalms 10, 19, 22, and 74.

Before protection, you may want to bless your space and yourself as well. Some say to bless after cleansing, but I would recommend blessing after protection.

The choice of when (or if) you bless is optional. Cleansing and protection are not.

Q: What about being hexed or cursed?

Usually, more serious cases do not happen out of nowhere. If you've invited or engaged with negative entities in any way, often they will hang around as they've been 'invited'. You can unknowingly have an entity attached to you, but these things do not happen without some kind of request from you.

Just as you would take showers regularly, the aura and energy in yourself and your home must be cleansed and protected with similar regularity.

Often *thinking* you are hexed or cursed *is* the curse.

In this state of thinking, any issue in a person's life can be a potential symptom of a curse, instead of regular life. Not only that, being overly concerned about whether or not someone has hexed you will put you in a state of being afraid, angry, and suspicious. In other words, just thinking you're hexed can put you in a personal state of hell.

Even if someone has cursed you, by getting worked up about it you are falling into the hex that was set. You create a mental condition that can be as difficult to remedy as an actual curse.

If no one has cursed you, then you've effectively cursed yourself. The best (and only) remedy for this is to live the happiest, most joy-filled life as possible.

No one can do anything to you that you don't allow, so do not worry about it.

Q: How do I know when my energy has been affected?

This requires some level of awareness. You need to know what your energy is like on a regular basis. Once you know who you are, it's easier to pick up on changes in your energy.

These unexplained changes are one clue that your energy has been affected and that it might be time for a deeper cleansing. Prolonged periods of emotional unrest are very common in the western world, to the point where many of us, unfortunately, believe it is normal to be hateful or cynical.

Peace and serenity are your natural state.

Any time you do not feel peace or serenity, your energy has been affected. Even if the reason you are affected emotionally is justified, your energy is still affected. This is one of the reasons many people will take extra good care of themselves whenever they're going through something troubling.

The short answer is: You'll know if your energy has been affected if you *feel* like your energy has been affected. The only way to know this is by bringing yourself to a calm and serene state. If you can't do this, that is one clue.

Cleansing Rituals and Spirit Washes

Being in a state of anger creates more anger. We all know someone who is just an angry person.

They always seem to be angry about the same things, or just angry wherever they go. This energy is a spirit. When something happens that annoys you, carrying anger with you afterward leaves you open to this spirit, and then vulnerable to all kinds of entities as your defenses are lowered.

In this section, we'll discuss the washes and methods that can be used to keep your aura and energy cleansed and protected.

Spiritually Cleansing the Home

Regularly cleaning your home isn't just about dusting and mopping. This is a ritual that many people do every weekend without thinking about the spiritual effects, beyond how it feels to have a clean space afterward.

As a regular practice you want to keep your home clear of clutter. If you already have some clutter in your home, this might seem like a daunting task, but it is a necessary one. You can start by taking this one step at a time.

Go through each room and make a pile of things you haven't used for a least a year, and then get rid of it.

Once you've cleaned your home of clutter, you can start on your first house cleaning. It doesn't matter if you've just moved in or have lived in the space for ten years.

A traditional hoodoo cleansing of the home starts in the uppermost corner, furthest away from the door. The walls are cleansed and washed first, and then the floor in each room.

For your wall and floors, you'll want to use a mixture made specifically for spiritually cleaning your home, such as a Chinese Wash (also called a Chinese Floor Wash).

This can be purchased at most hoodoo shops and can be diluted with some water. It does not need to be rinsed away, like a typical floor cleanser.

If you do buy anything from a curio shop that sells waters, consider putting 'you' into it, your saliva, blood, or nails.

When doing this type of cleaning, you want to use new, or clean rags, mops, and cleaning supplies.

While cleaning you want to pray over your space. This can come from your heart or you can recite a prayer specifically for purification and cleansing.

While going through your home you want to continuously state your intention by asking God to remove the negativity from your home. As you throw out and refill the warm water, state that negativity is permanently leaving your home now.

After cleaning each room, you can go straight to a protection prayer or ritual, or bless the space first. Blessing is moving through your home, in the same order that it was cleansed, and inviting love, peace, serenity, and any other good vibrations you want in. You can also sprinkle House Blessing oil as you go around to each room.

While you're blessing the home, you can also ask that *God and your guides lend their power to protecting your space*. However, most protection takes the form of having items in your home with the purpose of keeping negative energies away.

For Home Protection

There are countless ways you can protect your home and space, some more obvious than others. Really this is about helping you to *feel* protected, so if one method doesn't help you to feel protected in your home, try another one until the energy is right.

You can, of course, recite another Psalm specifically for protection: 14, 24, 29, 64, or 101.

After reciting the Psalm, you would make a statement of intention. Something that says the space is now protected from harmful entities and negative energy.

Another method of protecting your space is using a spray. Florida water is perhaps the simplest and easiest form of spiritual protection for your home. You can create your own spray using Holy Water, if you're able to access or purchase it.

If Holy Water isn't available to you, or you'd prefer to create your own cleansing spray, you can make one with some water (you can convert it to holy water from home, if you want) and some common ingredients from your kitchen.

Salt is one of these ingredients. The reason practitioners love it so much is because salt can do anything. Salt is like the clear quartz of your spice rack. Try a mix of consecrated salt and basil with water to create a home protection spray.

Dried herbs are great for protecting your home. You can hang an herb like basil to dry, and at the same time use it for keeping unwanted energies out of your space. You can also hang satchels of already dried herbs, like hyssop.

There are a number of items you can have in the home that will serve to protect your place. First: your plants! Specifically, cacti, orchids, ferns, snake plants, and ivy.

Chances are you probably have one of these in the home already. You can actually watch your plant as it grows and changes over the seasons. Start talking to your plants and share with them that you'd like their help in protecting where you all live.

If you are open to keeping a flame burning while you are at home, you can use the fire as a way to protect your space. Speak over the flame your intention and offer gratitude.

As an added boost of protection, you can place some crystals around the candle, such as black obsidian. Himalayan salt candle holders are widely available, and excellent for this purpose.

As mentioned, salt is all-purpose. Pink salt, specifically, is beneficial for filling your space with loving vibrations. It's also great for bringing prosperity to you.

In addition, the most powerful protector of your space is you. It is easy to overdo it when it comes to protection, which then underestimates your faith and the same power available to you.

When I mentioned above that you need to feel protected in your space, this isn't about using a spray or keeping a row of cacti on your windowsill. You decide if you feel protected or not, not the things you have in your home or the Florida Water you spray around. Feeling protected is a choice, do what you can to choose it. All of these methods are supposed to help you feel that.

Regular Cleaning and Protecting

Cleansing and protection need to happen regularly. There are many different methods for each. One of the most popular includes using fire and smoke.

This is a very popular way to cleanse your space. If you've ever burned sage, you're already familiar with how to do this. Usually, dried sage is burned loose inside of something called an abalone shell and wafted around using a large feather.

These leaves will often be available as a bundle, which makes it easier to carry around and wave around your space. You don't have to use a sage bundle for cleansing, however. You can make your own bundles for cleansing your space using pine or herbs.

Incense can be used to do both cleaning and protecting, as long as you use it with the right intention. There are lots of different types of incense, but as long as you get a high-quality one that was made for what you need, and you will be covered.

Resins like Frankincense and Myrrh are very popular for this purpose. These are burned on a charcoal disc, a round, black stone-looking thing that just needs a little fire to be lit. Usually, these are available in esoteric shops, or any place where you find incense.

Spiritually Cleansing the Body

It is very easy to carry negative energy with you in our current climate. As warped as it may sound, us living in the west are almost rewarded for living in fear, or by keeping our light hidden.

Many of the communities that make up life in our world are created around negativity; racism, homophobia, misogyny, misandry, transphobia, fatphobia, the list goes on. The truth is, in many cases these types of negative mindsets impact the people who think in these ways more than they affect the identified community.

This isn't all of it, there are seemingly a countless number of ways that your energy can be attacked. Mercury being in retrograde, for one.

Hoodoo Baths

If you were to see an experienced hoodoo practitioner, one of the first things they will most likely recommend to you (especially if you're not on a personal spiritual path) is a bath, but not the kind that we commonly see in commercials and on Instagram.

This kind of bath will usually involve collecting the tools and herbs we've discussed in the previous section. You may be asked to create a mixture with the intent of clearing your aura. If you're new to spiritual practices such as cleansing and protection, your spiritual body will be heavy *stuff* or baggage collected over your lifetime.

A mixture for cleansing will usually involve collecting a combination of roots like hyssop and rue, and Florida Water. There are mixtures (or 'dressings') that can be created for love, peace, healing, abundance, etc. They are often stirred around with each other, or literally cooked on a stove with prayers and petitions.

If you do have any allergies, test the ingredients on your skin individually prior to making the dressing and using it for a bath. The practitioner you're seeing will have more direction for you on this, depending on the working.

Once made, this dressing is usually rubbed on the body or put into a bath prepared for yourself. In the bath, you rub the roots and everything all over your body, into your skin and hair. Afterward, you'll most likely be instructed to keep the roots on your body as you air dry.

Baths like these can also be done outside, in a backyard for example if you are blessed enough to have access to one, or a space where you can be outside and have some privacy. In this case, you might take some of the mixture and rub it into your body, going from your toes to your head.

You might be tempted to get into the shower right away to rinse the debris off of you as in a typical bath or shower. It's important to follow the instructions of the practitioner you've hired exactly. It might feel awkward to have bits of rose petals in your nooks and crannies, but there's work happening. That's the important thing.

Will this make a mess? Yes. Will you get results? Definitely.

Hoodoo... Showers?

If you're not comfortable with the idea of a bath, a shower can be just as effective. Though, this isn't what's generally recommended in hoodoo, since with traditional baths, you're expected to really immerse yourself into the water with the prescribed ingredients you're using.

A shower version of a hoodoo bath can take place outside, as described above, or in your shower by just rubbing yourself down with the dressing. You would do the same thing as in a bath, just with a shower instead.

But your regular showers can serve double duty. Letting water run down your body isn't just an amazing experience, it can also take all of the things that you have collected and impacted your aura and wash them down the drain. You just have to speak it and make that intention known.

As with your home, after cleansing, you want to protect (and bless). Your form of protection may be using a lotion with an essential oil, like Frankincense. Blessing could be just anointing yourself with the oil by placing it on pressure points.

You'll also want to say a prayer or Psalms while you're blessing and protecting, a separate prayer for each, and then closing your blessing and protection with a statement of intention.

This is something that can be highly personal to you and your beliefs. If you're not sure how to do this or what to say at first, Psalms 23 is always a good option. You could also try: Psalms 19, 21, 24, 46, 65, 95, or 122.

You could also speak words over yourself. Remind yourself of your strength and power, your commitment to your path, or following inner guidance.

You might even be interested in my bother book called: "Prayers and Protection Magick to Destroy Witchcraft; Banish Curses, Negative Energy & Psychic Attacks; Break Spells, Evil Soul Ties & Covenants; Protect & Release Favors" -- as this book will give you many prayer options to recite and to add to your practice. You can find it at https://www.amazon.com/dp/B096W6J97R

For a deeper spiritual cleanse, you can use a number of common household items. Just like you can use salt to protect your home, you can use it for your body.

Mix some table or sea salt with coconut oil (though this can clog your drain, so be aware) for an in-shower scrub. Not only will you be able to get an exfoliation, a massage, and soft skin, but your energy will be clear. State your intention as you scrub and the dirt washes down the drain.

Soap

Many of the hoodoo oils you can find are also available as soaps, but there are some that are specific to the practice that are worth mentioning.

Sulfur soap is one example. If you're in need of a deep cleansing of negativity, washing with this soap every day will help. As with any product used on your skin, you'll want to test on a small section of your skin first.

Body Oil

There are many hoodoo oils created specifically to use on the body. These could be blessing oil, cut & clear, or psychic cleansing. These aren't the only oils you can use on your body, however. There are oils created specifically to attract love, abundance, good sex; almost anything you can think of.

You can use these oils to anoint yourself or add them to the washes and lotions you already use.

Body Powders

Some retailers offer hoodoo powders that can also be used in various ways. In most cases, these powders are used to hex someone else, by placing the powder in the path of the target.

However, you can find cleansing powders made from herbs that have been consecrated and prayed over. These powders can then be used as part of your cleansing rituals, so for example, you can use them to dress your candles. You can also add them to a mojo bag or add some onto a paper you've written a petition on.

Sweet Waters

As the name suggests, these waters can help to add some sweetness to your life or any of the situations that you want worked on.

These are made by using sweet substances, most often sweet herbs, sugar, and honey, but most ingredients with some sweetness will do, and of course the key ingredient: water. Baths with a sweet water can also typically include other ingredients like rose petals and holy water.

You'll most often find these used in spiritual baths, but they can also be used as offerings in rituals.

On the other hand, sour waters are made with sour ingredients such as vinegar and ammonia.

Fragrant Waters

These types of waters get their power from being used and *worked* with for many, many years. This means that many spirits have used and interacted with these waters before us, so by using them we create an association that spirits are familiar with.

These are also a common ingredient in baths, but you can also use them as a spray to cleanse and protect your aura or space.

Although Florida Water is a cologne, it is also considered a fragrant water. Other waters in this category include: Angel Water (also known as Portugal Water), Kananga Water, Rose Water.

Some of these types of waters are easy to make; you can also make substitutions. Rose Water is made using rose petals and enough distilled water to cover the petals (it's fine if some of them stay at the top of the water).

This combination is then boiled for about half an hour, and then strained to remove the petals.

If you don't have rose petals, you can use this same recipe to make other waters at home, such as lavender. If you don't have petals of any kind, an essential oil will do just fine, though be sure to use distilled water. Keep your homemade fragrant waters in the refrigerator.

Cleaning with Eggs and Crystals

A common method for cleaning in hoodoo is by using an egg, the same kind you might eat for breakfast. One egg is taken and rolled over the body. As this happens, it's said that the egg will absorb any negative energy. This can be done by going from the top of your head down to your feet.

Once this is complete, you can break the egg and flush it down a toilet. The egg would then have negative energy, and you don't want to keep those vibes hanging around.

Some crystals can be used in a way that is similar to the egg, but once cleansing is finished, your crystal needs to be cleared of the energy it absorbed. We'll go over this in Part III, Eradication and Getting Professional Help.

For Body Protection

Here's where you may want to carry a mojo bag, but as with home protection, there are *many* tactics you can use to protect yourself and your aura.

The simplest way to protect yourself, especially when you're out in public, is by carrying crystals. Many retailers on Etsy sell crystals as necklaces and bracelets. For most people, these pieces are sufficient for any and every situation.

If keeping crystals aren't your thing, try using a bay leaf. Charge it by praying to the leaf and asking for protection and carrying it on you.

Prayers are very effective in protecting your energy. Say one while you're at home in the same way you would bless yourself. You can also use protective prayers and mantras as you're out or whenever you feel like you need extra protection.

Repeating verses from Psalms can work for this, or by saying something like: *I claim divine protection as my birthright. I am now balanced and centered.*

On Knowing You Are Protected

In the same way that you have to claim protection over your home, you have to claim protection over yourself. Thinking that you are 'vulnerable' and 'in need of protection' will lead you to being vulnerable and in need of protection.

It can be difficult to trust that you are protected at first, because it doesn't feel like it should be that easy; to be protected by just claiming that you are protected. This goes back to your faith in God, and, by extension, your faith in yourself, the power of your word.

Things can always happen to you physically. This is just a fact of being human; our bodies are 3D and thereby frail. Your job, and my job, *our* job is to correctly identify who we are and what we are. What we are not, is these frail, itchy bodies.

You may have heard this line before, but it bears repeating: we are spiritual bodies in a physical experience. If you've never taken the time to think about what this means, consider this the moment.

You can cast spells for physical protection, but if you're not in a situation where there is immediate danger, I encourage you to not worry about the potential ways you can be physically hurt in the world.

It is *very* easy to undermine your own power when it comes to the concept of protection, especially of the body. Let's take two people who say in their morning prayer: *I claim divine protection over my mind, body, and spirit now.*

The first person says the statement and then charges a crystal necklace with those words and anoints their mojo bag. Throughout the day they repeat the statement and touch their mojo bag whenever they feel threatened. They touch the bag when it looks like a stranger is getting close to them, and in their car on the way to work.

At the end of the day, they may realize they were safe and protected, nothing happened that actually put them in danger, but then in their mind they negate that thought by thinking something could happen tomorrow and making a statement to themselves that sounds like "people are crazy".

The other person says that statement, takes a moment to actually claim it, and then goes about their day never thinking or wondering if they're protected. Their day looks a lot like the first person's, but they know they are protected even when a barking dog rushes towards them on an afternoon walk.

To be clear: I am *not* saying one approach is "right" and one is "wrong". Both approaches are "right". The first person is doing amazing work to help themselves *feel* protected. This work must be recognized. Eventually, if they keep their practices up, they will have less of a need for them and may come to some awareness about how their own thoughts are creating their reality.

My point with this example is to demonstrate what it can look like when a person tells themselves one thing but contradicts that with their actions. The person who tells themselves they are protected but then throughout a day feels they need protection especially where there is no real "danger", proves to themselves the opposite. They prove to themselves that they are *not* protected.

Likewise, the person who says *I am protected* and then behaves as such is training themselves to believe their own word. They effectively are protected simply because they claim that for themselves as truth.

What we're talking about here is the power of your tongue. As Proverbs 18:21 says: *The tongue has the power of life and death*. If you're trying to create a condition in your experience, you are trying to bring something 'to life'.

You might be trying to bring love into your life, or more money, or luck ahead of a game. On the other hand, there are probably conditions in your life that you are trying to wipe away or banish. If you want love, the thing you want to banish might be loneliness.

This verse from Proverbs means that the words you use can either make these things happen or leave you in a life where you're constantly searching for what you want. The person who believes themselves when they say *I am divinely protected* has brought protection to life in their experience using their words.

The person who says they are divinely protected, but then says things in contradiction with that statement, brings to life a conflicted experience. They feel protected when they pray or touch their mojo bag, but then they say something to themselves that causes them to feel vulnerable (like "people are crazy").

I see this often with new practitioners who have been victims of physical abuse or violence. Growing up in a violent household can leave us scarred for life, and constantly worrying about when the next attack is going to come is one of the ways these scars can show up.

This worrying, as we've covered, is another spell--a curse, specifically, one that you can cast on yourself.

This is one of the reasons self-love and self-respect are so important. You have to love yourself enough to not tolerate any self-bullying.

Your spiritual practice and hoodoo can help you to heal these scars. You do have to be willing to give up the pain. It is hard work, but it's harder to live in fear and pain, in my opinion. So, if you're going to have a difficult time, why not just put your effort towards believing in your own power?

Chance is a natural part of the human experience. At the same time, it *is* natural for you to be at peace, healthy, and wealthy at all times. You can claim protection just by claiming your birthright as a peaceful, healthy, and prosperous human being.

Staying Protected

Connect with your divinity now. Say to yourself: *I connect with my higher self and divine spirit now*, and then give yourself a few moments to actually connect.

Then check in with how you feel.

Do you feel like you need protection in this state? If the answer is yes, then you know that protection is yours without needing anything else. The crystals and mojo you use to that end are to *help* you maintain this feeling.

You feeling protected is the key ingredient here. Without this, nothing you buy or create will work for you. If you can imagine that you're not safe, you can also imagine that the powerful tools at your disposal can't or won't work.

From that you have created a curse on yourself, and if you're constantly in fear or anger. One of the ways this 'self-curse' can show up in your life is through sickness or illness. At the very least, claiming protection as your birthright protects you from the assault on your immune system that can result from a fear-based idea or thoughtform.

Fires, Candles, and Incense Rites

Fire is cleansing. It has the power to shed light on everything and burn it all away-the good and the bad. Which means handling fire requires extra care. There are multiple ways you can use fires and candles in your daily practice.

You can simply talk to a candle. If there's anything that is troubling you or heavy on your mind, go to your altar and just make a practice of talking to the candle. Bring any problems or issues you have to the flame and then when you leave, imagine your problem has been burned away.

Don't forget to express your gratitude to the spirit of the fire.

Fire can also be used to protect, if used carefully.

A rite, in hoodoo, is a simple practice that is not quite a spell and not quite a ritual. It can be done every day, once over a week, or any other regular interval. An example of a simple fire rite is burning cloves in your home to remove your space of negative or harmful energies.

Rites are also often accompanied by a repeated prayer or affirmation.

Smoke cleansing is very popular in many Indigenous cultures around the world. Smoke was also used to summon spirits and to heighten the energy in a space.

This is taking the herbs or leaves that you are burning and lighting them in a heatproof dish. Many practitioners use an abalone shell, but any heat-resistant dish will do, but it has to be one that you can carry if you're going to smudge an area with different rooms, like your home.

Walk around with the smoking leaves and incense and use a feather to gently waft the smoke around the area.

As you're doing this, you can recite a Psalms or state what you want. This might sound something like: *I invite God's light into this space right now. Cleanse this space of any negative entities or energies.*

You can continue going back and forth in the space until whatever your burning has gone out, or until you feel like the space is cleared. Your intuition will tell you when this is.

We're a little more accustomed to using fire as a form of magick in everyday life. This is what it means to blow out candles on a birthday cake! But we also light candles to change the energy in a space, such as creating a romantic environment on Valentine's Day.

Another simple rite is lighting a candle, possibly one dressed with an oil and some herbs, and reciting a blessing as the light burns. To 'bless' something can be simply saying that you bless the item or substance you're using.

To bless a candle, you could cleanse it first, and then say over it: *I bless this candle by my own power.* You can also recite Psalms 23 over the dressed candle. It really can be this simple.

Going back to the power of your word, your breath also has power. This is why many practitioners do not blow candles out, particularly for magick used to bring things to you.

With magick to rid yourself of things or to cleanse, it's fine to blow out a candle as this can represent putting out the condition in your life.

You can pull into yourself fire energy. Some spiritual practices believe that every human has fire within them, represented by our ability to will ourselves to make things happen.

A safety tip. If you're doing a spell that requires burning anything and keeping the ashes, most practitioners use a cauldron, but if you don't have one, you can use tin foil. Just set the foil down on top of whatever plate or dish you're using and keep the fire burning on top. This gives you an easy way to collect ashes.

For Spell Casting

Before you can cast an authentic spell, there are a few concepts that we need to cover. First, spells are everywhere. Many practitioners consider the bible itself to be a spellbook.

Mantras are spells, as are the songs we listen to or music videos we watch. In this broader context there isn't really a process for casting a spell; they happen all of the time and often without our knowledge.

It's when you want to cast a spell with intention and with the help of Spirit that the work we've discussed gets involved. In previous chapters, we've mentioned bits and pieces of the process. Here's where we put it all together.

Living a Magickal Life: Before You Begin

You have to have the right energy. In Part One I described a worker who started clearing out their space even before they casted a spell. I'm going to continue with this example to describe how you want to create an energetic environment that will make your space conducive to doing work.

Getting rid of clutter is one way you can do this in your home (since this is where most work happens).

You want to make both your physical and your spiritual environments as clear as possible before casting a spell. This is why many workers do activities (rites and rituals) on a daily basis that keep them aligned, their space clear, and their connection with spirit strong.

I can't really prescribe what this will look like for you, your daily practice will be dictated by your relationship with spirit.

Your practice could involve elements of hoodoo and other magickal practices. This could look like exercising and meditating daily, speaking to your ancestors and speaking to the roots, and keeping a careful watch of your plants. You may sage your apartment or spray around a homemade cleansing water every week. Once in a while you might incorporate regular visits to a cemetery near your home where you leave coins at the gate. This is just an example.

The point is living a magickal life means that when it comes time to work, you're not completely starting from scratch. You will have started and built a strong relationship with Spirit and with your ancestors already, *before* you start your spell.

Pro Tip: Turn on the music! Your favorite music is an *excellent* way to build the right energy in your space before casting a spell. Anything that helps you to feel like your spirit is lifted and keeps your vibration high.

This is all about your preference. Music with lyrics might be distracting, or they could help you. Put together a playlist before starting your next spell.

What are you Saying?

Another thing you may want to prepare prior to starting your spell is knowing exactly what you're going to say, especially if you don't feel confident making prayers and statements of edification to spirit.

It's completely normal to feel nervous, but you also have to remember that *you* are a spiritual being as well.

The energies you are calling in are Spirit. They already know they are being called in to help you. Spirit is always with you. Breathe, get yourself to a calm and centered state, and remember your intention.

You won't completely ruin everything if you forget to do something or stumble on your words. Remember: Spirit understands *your intent*, first and foremost.

The Phases of a Spell

Most work happens in a sequence of phases. Generally, you open a spiritual channel, welcome the spirits that will help you, and communicate with them while working with your tools.

Keep in mind: each practice has a different way to complete each phase. Another practitioner might start with a smudge to cleanse their space and then use a wand to cast a circle. This circle is used to protect themselves as they open the energy to the spirit dimension.

After this, they will call the spirits from the four directions. This is one example of a common way spells are cast amongst witches in the Wicca tradition.

Phase #1: Incense, light, and water. Your first step in casting a spell is lighting a candle and having an offering, such as a glass of water, with you in your working space. This is so that when you call the spirits you're working with, they can see their way to you and are welcomed with your offering.

Before your spell, you may also want to consider using incense (in addition to the candle) to invite spirit into your space. More on this later.

In some types of spells, you want to use a candle of a specific color. Protection spells, for example, often call for black candles. Some of the spells below indicate what color of candle you will want to use.

Phase #2: Offering. Give something to the spirits you're inviting to help you with the work. As discussed in previous sections, this could be a song you sing, cigar smoke, incense smoke, etc.

Phase #3: The four directions. All magick honors north, south, east, and west in some way. These directions are also associated with the elements; earth, fire, wind, and water, respectively.

It is expected that before your work begins, you 'present' the herbs you are working with to the four directions. This will look like taking the ingredients in your hands and holding them up towards each direction with focus and intention.

For this phase, you might want to have a special dish you use specifically for herbs and roots. Otherwise, you can put some of the ingredients in your hand.

Phase #4: Your intention and prayers. This is where you pray over the herbs and say what it is you want for the work. In hoodoo, the bible is almost exclusively used for this.

At first you might want to start with the Psalms, but there are many chapters and books of the bible that can be used as prayers. You also want to speak from your heart, ensuring that you acknowledge the spirits involved and your ancestors.

Here's what this might sound like for a prosperity working. *Thank you, ancestors! Thank you for being here as I set out to do this work. I am ready to embrace prosperity in my life in all forms. I know that you are here with me, that I do this standing on the foundation you have laid before me. And with the power and strength you've given me, I ask that the spirit contained in these roots come to my aid. This work is to give life to financial blessings, success, money, new clients who pay on time, and are happy to do so. To the spirits of these roots: let it be so.*

Key Considerations. There is a time and a season for everything, magick included. Casting a spell requires a bit of planning.
- *Time of the month*. Spells for drawing something to you should be done during the waxing moon phase, usually a couple days after the new moon and a couple days before the full moon. A couple days after the full moon you can do banishing magic; any magick with the intent to ridding your life of some condition.
- *Day of the week*. Whether or not this is as important as time of the month is up for debate, but each day of the week is ruled by an energy and a spirit.
- *Time of day*. You don't have to get down to the hour and minute, but there are certain 'magickal' times of day.
- *Your notes*. Keep a note of all of the above considerations, plus the ingredients you use (you can copy from this book, but likely you'll have substitutions) and anything you felt before, during, and after the spell. This can be in the same notebook you use to keep track of your roots and herbs supply.

For each of the spells in this section, you will gather the herbs and ingredients listed and plan out when to do the working based on the key considerations.

Give yourself enough time to gather everything and consecrate what you're using.

Spells for Keeping the Peace

There are many situations where you may need extra help with maintaining peace, either within yourself or your home. Just thinking of our current climate will probably provide you with a long list.

Before gathering your ingredients and writing your petition, it is important to know why the spell is necessary. With technology taking over more and more aspects of our lives, it seems stress and anxiety have risen exponentially.

I'm not going to get into the how's and why's too much, but in short, most of the apps and services we use on our phones are designed to make us feel like if we're not staring at the screen, we're missing out on something.

Many people are dealing with illnesses of all kinds. We know that stress and anxiety can either make you sick or worsen your health. In this case, keeping the peace can then have a direct effect on your health and your wealth.

While you might not feel the stress and anxiety of living in these modern times, or your health may be in check, the people you live with could be susceptible to any of these pressures. This will affect you and the energy in your space.

Often in homes where there are regular disturbances, in the form of abuse or addiction, there are *many* problems. The larger issue will trigger a domino effect, one that you can protect yourself against with the right perspective, and a little magick.

After your work is complete, you can do your best to know that peace is yours, regardless of what's going on around you. If you do your work and then continue to worry about whatever your situation, you are not practicing faith.

Continuing to feel anxiety or entertain thoughts of worry will not only reverse your work, but it will also lead you to cast another spell, then another, then another.

Once you cast your spell for peace, know that it *worked*.

Following your spell, you may find it helpful to use rituals with the intention of maintaining peace in your space. This is where you can use prayers, incense, essential oils like tea tree, or crystals. Below you'll find some waters, dirt, and minerals that are helpful to bring peace where ever you go.

For Home: A Candle Spell

This simple candle spell is designed to keep peace in your home. You will need:

1. A white or blue candle.
2. A candle holder or plate that will hold the candle as it burns.
3. House Blessing oil (you can use olive oil as a substitute, just be sure to consecrate it first).
4. Choose what you can from the following (use what you have on hand): basil, cilantro, coffee, coriander, or rosemary.
5. Rose or lavender petals.
6. A plate for the herbs and petals.
7. A plain piece of paper to write a peace petition on.

Instructions

Arrange the herbs and petals on the plate, with the candle and oil (still in the bottle). Pray over everything and consecrate using Psalms.

Write your petition down on the paper. While writing, imagine that the protection you are requesting is already done. Include all the names of the people in your household, if applicable, or your name.

If the paper is large and needs to be folded or ripped, do this action *towards* yourself. This is to signify drawing the protection energy towards you. (Conversely, if you are using a petition for a banishing spell, you would rip or fold away from you.)

Dress the candle with the oil, while instructing it what you want to do. Feel the energy flow through your hands and into the wax as you chant. Once the candle is dressed with oil, place it in its holder.

Dress the candle with the herbs and petals, again chanting and providing direction. Light the candle seeing your spell come to life.

Leave the candle burning for as long as possible. If you have to leave the candle unattended, snuff it out. Never blow it out (blowing out a candle is better for banishing magick).

For Your Space: A Knot Spell

The first at-home spell is fine if you live in a home where others know what you do and you can work without judgment or disturbances.

In other words, your whole home may be a safe space for you to practice magick. *Many* of the talented and powerful practitioners I know started their practice as teenagers, in homes where their parents or guardians were not supportive of their practice, if not downright hostile.

If you have at least a private space where you can practice, you can build the energy of peace within; a type of field that is protective and where you are in control.

Keep in mind that all of the materials used are there to represent spirit. In your private space, you can connect with any spirit without needing a physical root or seed.

This will require you to build some of your powers, like visualization. Some practitioners I've spoken to who used magick in tough situations consider their time in difficulty a gift for this reason. It forced them to become adept at their magick without relying on anything but their ancestors and guides.

Taking care of yourself and building your personal magickal power becomes even more important in this case. The more peace you can feel *before* doing the spell, the more effective it will be.

Of course, one of the best tools you can use in this situation would be a bible, if you have one. If you don't have one, you can find any book and chapter you need free online.

For this spell I'm going to assume you don't want anything that involves fire, smoke, or produces an odor. Do not think that these conditions mean you're limited in any way. With just a few roots and herbs, you can still do workings like mojo bags and spell jars. You can also use string for knot magic, which is the spell I'm going to describe below.

This spell is about 'tying' yourself and your space to the spirit of peace.

You will need:
1. String in a 'peace' color (see candle options above) or any type of string that is strong enough to withstand being tied into knots (i.e. not sewing thread). Twine is an excellent, neutral option.
2. Your petition and statements.

Instructions

Cut your string long enough so you can tie nine knots, and then double this over so you have one end that is a loop.

This spell is really about item #2. You want to have your intention so clear in your mind, that when speaking freely your words match up with what you want. This spell is about solidifying what you want as your hands tie each knot.

Tie three knots, close together making your statements. Then three more, and then the last three doing the same.

Your petition does not have to be the same for each knot. For example, for the first knot in this spell you may say something as simple as: *Peace now for me and my space*. The second knot: *Serenity now for me and my space*. The third: *Inner stillness for me and my space*.

If you need to be even quieter, you can say these in your mind, pray or meditate on what you want.

After your first nine knots are tied, continue to make ties until your string becomes a ball of ties. This is an optional step, but if your knots are broken or untied for any reason, that is in effect undoing the spell.

This means that if your string breaks, you will have to start again. This is why you'll double up the string before starting the spell; to better protect from breaking the string.

For Work: A Jar Spell

With more of us working from home than ever before, you may think a spell for peace in the home is enough to create peace in your work environment. For many people, the workplace and the home remain separate, and even if you do work from home, we know how important boundaries are.

In either case, a spell to encourage peace in the workplace may be necessary because of your manager or co-workers.

This spell is designed to be contained inside of a small, glass jar. You can use the same herbs and ingredients as I listed in the spell for your home. Aside from that, will need:

1. A glass jar small enough to keep at work or in the office.
2. A candle, keeping color correspondences in mind.
3. Seashells.
4. Sugar, brown or white will work fine.
5. Juniper berries.
6. Lavender essential oil.

If you have someone at the workplace who is particularly difficult to deal with, add a conjure oil to the recipe. You could include a Clarity, Stop Gossip, or Tranquility oil as part of your jar, but keep in mind how long you intend to keep the work for.

Jars can be used to improve a condition over a long or short period of time. With the wrong oil or ingredient, you could end up doing magick that could create unwanted results over time. Usually, this warning would be for any type of banishing magick. Keep the intention here clear: for peace in the workplace.

Instructions

Go through the four phases of your spell with your materials and ingredients. Once you're ready to put your jar together, charge each item before putting it inside by using your words and breath. Breathe your intention into each item and be specific about why you're adding it to your jar.

For example, for the seashell you might say: *Bring peace and tranquility to this spell, and to this work now and in perpetuity.*

Once you've finished adding all of your items, speak your intention into the jar one last time before closing it. Depending on the size of the jar, you can burn the candle on top of it or on a plate nearby.

If you're using one of the 4-inch candles that are common in magickal practice, you can stick it to the top of your jar by melting some of the wax on the bottom and holding it in place until the wax hardens.

Light the candle and let it burn out on top of the jar. You can also burn some of the wax around the lid of the jar to 'seal' it, but this is up to you.

Once you've made the jar, you have to 'work' the magick to keep the energy going. There are many ways to do this, but the simplest is to shake the jar while repeating your petition. It doesn't have to be the same one you used while creating the work; it can be whatever speaks to the intent.

Peace Rituals: Using Waters

Following your candle spell, an excellent way to maintain the peace in your home is by using waters. These can be sprinkled around your home, room to room in a clockwise manner. Start in the room furthest from the door and start by standing towards the west.

As you sprinkle, use your voice to ask the waters for what you want. You can say something like: *I invite peace and serenity in this space now*. Or just repeat words to conjure what you want, such as: *peace, serenity, love, harmony*.

With any rite, you want to feel gratitude and the peace that you want in your environment within yourself. Express gratitude to your ancestors and the spirit of the waters for responding to your requests.

Peace Water is perhaps the most obvious for this purpose. This, as well as all of the waters listed here, can be placed in spray bottles for a convenient peace spritz whenever you need it.

This type of water is great for calming the energy in your home down after chaos or following the visit from anyone suffering from an illness.

If you'd prefer a water that has more varied properties, you really cannot go wrong with **Florida**

Water. It is so popular across many magickal traditions, that you can now find it at some retailers as soap or hand sanitizer.

Gardenias Cologne. Can be used in a way similar to Peace Water, described above.

Lavender Cologne. Excellent if you're in a marriage or love relationship with someone you live with.

Cold Water. The type that comes out of a tap. Using a bowl of cold water, you can sprinkle *coolness* and *calmness* around your home or your workspace. This option works best if you are sensitive to smells, or live or work around others who are also sensitive.

Peace Rituals: Using Dirt and Minerals

I mentioned using **dirt from a church** in a mojo bag for love, but this can also be used to bring peace to your home or place of work (if these two spaces aren't one and the same).

Chalk or **Cascarilla** (pronounced kaws-kuh-ree-uh). An inexpensive powder made of eggshells that can be added to workings or sprinkled around a space.

Peace Powder. Sometimes this is the same as Cascarilla, but you can also find botanicals that make unique blends. For use in the home or at work.

Spells for Attraction, Love, and Relationships

Attraction, love, relationships, sex, and marriage are among the top reasons people either figure out how to do a spell on their own or hire a conjurer. If you've gone down either of these paths and what you wanted to happen didn't, it can be an incredibly frustrating experience.

The difficulty here is that often this magick is about controlling someone else's behavior. This is where it can become dangerous to have our minds set so fixedly on someone else, that we lose sight of the one truth of being human: that we all have free will.

However, love hoodoo is best used in situations where the emotions and love are there, but just need some assistance. Trying to cast a spell on someone who has never even looked your way only sets your work up for a very likely failure.

The same goes for spells cast on someone or for a situation where another person has not expressed any interest, or they've said they are not interested at all. Of course, it is possible to continue casting spells until your intended changes their mind, but these types of stories rarely end well.

It's for this reason that you want to cast a love spell with your first eye open. Are you using the spell to draw a specific person to you? And if so, is there a difference between the love you are fantasizing about and what it would be like in real life?

But in the case that you already have someone in your life that you are deeply in love with, hoodoo is excellent for strengthening that relationship and making it even stronger.

For Heating up Your Love Life: An Apple Spell

Apples are very common in love spells in hoodoo and some European magickal traditions. This spell is to heat up a relationship and add some passion to your love.

It is meant to draw these things to your relationship, and so I would recommend doing it during a waxing moon phase (after the new moon, before the full moon).

You will need:

1. An apple, fresh. Choose one that can stand evenly. You'll be putting the candle into the apple and you don't want to risk it tipping over.
2. A four-inch candle.
3. Coriander seeds.
4. Ginger root.
5. Marjoram.
6. Rose petals.

7. Sugar.
8. Love Me or a Marriage conjure oil.
9. A magnet.
10. Magnetic sand.
11. A photo of you and your partner.
12. A plate.
13. A bowl filled with holy or consecrated water.

You can use substitutions for many of the ingredients. Lavender petals can work instead of rose, but you want to know what each type of flower will bring to your work (meaning, what kind of results you can expect using one flower in substitution for another). Try to get fresh flowers.

Instructions

Keep the photo of you and your partner nearby, preferably somewhere you can see it while you're doing the following steps.

Stick the candle in at the top and press down just enough so it sticks out of the apple. Start your spell by speaking to the apple. Turn it clockwise while speaking your intention and desires into its skin and essence. Imagine your words going right into the seeds of the apple.

Place the apple in the middle of the plate. Anoint it with your hoodoo oil, again being sure to say what the work is for and what it is that you want. Next, place the magnet beside the apple on a side nearest to you. Sprinkle the magnetic sand on top. Now it's ready to be dressed.

Dress the apple by laying the coriander seeds, ginger root, marjoram, and sprinkle your sugar around it in a clockwise motion (to indicate drawing this hot energy to you and your relationship). Place the rose petals around next. Do this with intention. Take each item in your hand and connect with the spirit. After putting it around the apple, sprinkle some on top of the water in the bowl (including the rose petals).

Try to arrange everything on the plate with enthusiasm and creativity; take your time and make it appear pleasing to yourself.

Really feel the roots and plants that you're using. Touch and smell, imagine the heat, good feelings, and beauty being the same as in your relationship.

Every emotion you have while doing the work will show up in your magic, so make it count.

Light the candle, again with your intentions and prayers. As the flame burns, express gratitude! Thank the spirits for helping you with your work and being with you to see your spell come to life.

You will use the water to bathe with over the next few days. If you are working with a deity, choose a number of days that correspond with the spirit.

Three is a number often chosen because it represents a holy trinity; father, sun, and the holy spirit, or Father God, Mother Goddess, and you.

History Traditions of Hoodoo Love Magic

If you've ever watched daytime talk television, you know exactly the kinds of situations folks used to go to hoodoo for. Love triangles, cheaters, unrequited love, getting dumped, wandering eyes, jealousy, loneliness, lust, sex, getting pregnant, getting others to stop interfering in a relationship, removing a third party, triggering a breakup (either for someone else or for yourself), the list is probably endless.

When it comes to magick, society used to be much more forgiving when it comes to questions of love. Advertisements for love potions were common in magazines and pamphlets in the 1920s and 30s.

A very special spirit many hoodoo practitioners have used for nearly 100 years to draw success in many areas in life, but particularly love, is called a 'lodestone'.

For love, you can get two stones; female/male, or male/male, female/female (depending on the retailer).

Although you can find these in crystal or metaphysical shops, these are not treated in the same way as your regular crystals or stones, like lapis lazuli or clear quartz. At least not in the hoodoo tradition.

Regardless of whether you get a pair for your relationship, or one to draw love to you, lodestones are more like pets than they are a crystal. They require care in a way unique from other stones to 'activate' them and their work for your situation.

As a beginner, your best bet may be to consult an expert about how to care for your lodestone since they will know how to program your stone for your situation.

As many stories as there are about how hoodoo was used for love in years gone by, there are cautionary tales. For example, a man who had a love powder that he wanted to give to a woman he loved but didn't love him.

After she refused to eat the working (which was put in a slice of watermelon), he gave the food to some hogs. If he wasn't sure that the powder would work, he got confirmation because the hogs fell in love and ended up following him around![2]

---

[2] Hyatt, H. M. (1970). Hoodoo, Conjuration, Witchcraft, Rootwork. Five Volumes (1st ed.). Self-published, 1970s.

Then there are ways, using nature and communicating with spirit, to get answers to burning questions (or just simmering questions). Some of these tactics more dangerous than others. One method describes using knot magick; taking a string with a knot in it and having the couple pull each side. If the knot remains after being pulled, the two in love are in effect, 'tied together'.

Cautions and warnings in hoodoo love spells are just as old as the spells themselves. While we may not see advertisements for spells in our popular magazines and television shows, this work is real, that much we know.

However, no retailer can guarantee results in every situation. And without the right care and attention, unexpected results happen all the time.

Not all magick is used to cause changes in a situation. Sometimes, lighter spells and rituals are performed to find out where someone's heart lies. This doesn't mean that we approach spirit with a nonchalant attitude. Balance must be considered, as well as the potential for unintended consequences.

Making and Maintaining a Love Mojo

A mojo bag is perfect for those who are hoping to draw love into their lives. You are supposed to already feel like you have love in your life. Feeling desperate or 'thirsty' indicates not being connected to your higher self.

You cannot feel desperate *and* be the magnetic, attractive person you are supposed to be. The two ideas do not go together.

With a mojo bag to draw love, you can connect to your inner magnetism. You can sit back and watch your love options be drawn to you, and then choose amongst the people who want to give you their heart. All you have to do is keep your eyes (and heart) open.

However, if right now you *feel* desperate to find someone, you will have to do your best to undo this way of thinking *first*. Before you decide to do a love working of any kind. Consider doing a self-love spell or building a relationship with your ancestors with the intention of getting help.

Not all mojo bags need to be maintained, but regularly feeding a mojo bag keeps the work working. This is important in love, especially as you may date many people and might need the hand for some time before you find someone you want to settle down with.

Or your love mojo bag may be about a way of life for you and not necessarily about finding someone to settle down with. It all depends on your intent.

If you're creating a mojo bag for a relationship, you want to have elements inside that connect to both you and your partner. This could be toenail clippings or hair from both of you.

This bag is a living, breathing spirit itself.

Once your mojo bag is created, you can feed it by anointing it with conjure oils or essential oils. This is placing a few drops of the oil on your hand and then on the bag, the specific spots being completely up to you. You can also leave your mojo bag on your altar and present offerings, in the same way you would with other spirits.

How often you do this is up to you. One easy way to plan how often you do this and when is to schedule around moon cycles.

Feel free to start with one of the mojo bag recipes in the section above, keeping in mind that your intent and your feeling are key.

Once it's made and you've had the bag for at least a week, maintaining the bag is a process of anointing it regularly, and adding mojo. This is literally opening the bag and adding ingredients, like you are literally feeding it. Ritualize this. Light incense and build your energy using music or your body. Keep your vibration high and your intention front of mind.

The specific oils you want to use for anointing will have to be high-quality conjuring oils. For this you may not want to go with a love oil, rather a Blessing or Abramelin Oil. This is about feeding your bag, which helps you with your mojo. Your intent isn't about what you want, this is about putting energy into the bag. This is about praising and uplifting the spirits aiding your mojo.

Aromatherapy for Hoodoo Love

Incense, colognes, oils, and perfumes. In case you were beginning to think scents are important in hoodoo, you would be correct. Scents are valuable in many magickal traditions.

Aromatherapy provides a simple and quick method to welcome spirits into your space. It's also a way to either change or lift vibrations ahead of a ritual or casting a spell.

One common way to do this is through the use of incense. Other forms of aromatherapy are through using essential oils in a diffuser, burning resins such as frankincense or copal (which is especially good for love work), cones and sticks.

Burning sage and palo santo are generally used for cleansing, but these are also forms of aromatherapy that open up your space to the invitation of spirit.

Your words work in the same way that smoke does, it floats up into the air and goes somewhere that becomes invisible to the human eye.

Spirits are attracted to spaces with good, clear energy (or at least the spirits that you want to invite to help you). Using aromatherapy will clear the way for your appeals and prayers.

Many people who practice hoodoo consider using an incense essential ahead of any spell.

Because of its ability to completely change the vibration of a space, aromatherapy is excellent when it comes to love. Burn some incense after an argument and ask that spirits lift you up or ease the tension. You could also use an essential oil like rosemary or lavender.

A simpler method to easing the mood in your home is by boiling one or two cinnamon sticks in water.

One practice many in hoodoo and witchcraft are familiar with is creating custom incenses. Be sure that by knowing the magickal correspondences of various herbs, roots, oils, and plants, you can become your own aromatherapist with a background in magick.

This means you can create incenses to fill your home with the mood of love, to dispel anger, or for reconciliation. Note that some magickal suppliers sell these incenses pre-made.

For some, creating an incense *is* the spell. Common tools for creating an incense or a mortar and pestle to mix ingredients, and a cauldron to light the incense.

While burning, you can use the smoke and the energy of the spirits to do work. You can think about what it is that you want, breathing in and out deeply. You can say your intention and send it in the air along with the smoke.

Don't think that the activities you do need to be highly complicated or ritualistic. Let the smoke do the work for you and allow your vibration to be carried upwards. You can write a letter to the person you're thinking of, if, for example, your relationship is fractured, or you have a lot of intense feelings.

You can also praise and rejoice! If you have been doing other spells to bring love into your life, light some incense, invite the spirits helping you with your work in, and dance and sing. Conjure the feeling that what you want has already happened and what you want will come to you even faster.

Spells for Money, Luck, Abundance, and Prosperity

The second most popular reason many people pursue hoodoo, is for work with the intention of improving an employment or career situation.

Hoodoo is great for any type of employment, whether you're working for yourself or someone else.

There are spells for nearly every aspect of your business that you can imagine, getting along better with coworkers or a boss, attracting clients, drawing more money to you, side gigs, finding work or finding new work, or changing any condition with your employment.

Some conjure oils for work include: Boss Fix, I Can, You Can't, Road Opener, and Steady Work. These oils might not be available at all retailers, but keep in mind you can create your own.

Most of us would not be surprised to know that money, success, and prosperity have their own spirit. You can make you and your environment attractive to these spirits, or you can repel them. The unfortunate thing is often we don't *know* when we've made ourselves unattractive to the spirit of money.

What the richest members of our society know is that wealth is an attitude, a vibration. It is something that everyone is free to choose, like any other. What follows, then, is that an attitude of poverty is also a vibration and is also a choice.

This isn't to say that those of us who are rich always have a prosperous mindset, or the other way around.

The problem is when a person wants more money or success, but they don't have the right attitude for it. This is literally a roadblock that will stop your chances before you even set out to start.

The good news is that you can use hoodoo to help yourself out of a contradictory attitude, so that the results from the work you do for more money or a better career will have a clear channel.

That being said, you might wonder about magick to stop other people from getting in your way. My response is, there isn't so much a concern about others in your way than there is energy.

Hoodoo cannot change fate; no magick can.

If there's a job you want that you aren't qualified for, no amount of incense or mojo will give you more experience or education. Preparing yourself puts you in a good position to see results in your work, but success requires balance.

The point about fate also points to the question of your life path, specifically the work you want to put out into the world and how you want to make money. Sometimes the obstacles in your way are there because the path you're walking is not quite right for you.

I see this often, working with clients who have conformed their nature to work in corporate environments, when in reality they crave a life of creativity and freedom that is inconsistent with working in an office.

They go from job to job, punishing themselves for not being more grateful that they've been able to find work, but miserable, nonetheless. Which only makes them feel even worse.

This is one of the issues that highlights the value of a close relationship with your ancestors, and the value of knowing who you are. Once you have these in place, any work you do for success will be very, very powerful.

A Jar Spell to Make Money Sweet on You

Earlier we went over a jar spell for peace in the workplace. Here, we'll cover another version of this spell: to help make money sweet on you. This one you don't have to keep in the workplace, it can stay in your home or on a money altar. For this spell, we'll go a little more in-depth than with the others. For the most part, I've tried to list items that are common in most homes.

Items from Your Pantry
- Sugar
- Honey
- Cinnamon
- Coffee* (especially if you drink regularly or daily)
- Rosemary
- Bay Leaves
- Thyme
- Star Anise*
- Peppermint
- Bee Pollen

Crystals
- Clear Quartz
- Citrine
- Bismuth (optional, see below)
- Pyrite

Curios
- Coins (stick to a certain number, denomination doesn't matter, but if you have coins from another country, feel free to use those).
- Dirt from the land around a bank or financial district in your neighborhood.
- A bill of some denomination (ditto re: foreign currency).

- Thread (green, though orange or purple could work).

Materials
- Candle of your choice.
- Marker (blue or green, but black will do fine).
- Incense of some kind to clear and raise energy.
- A plate for the work.

For the materials I would encourage you to get something from the natural environment in your neighborhood. In my area, helicopter seeds cover the sidewalks in the spring and into summer. You may have access to a garden or wooded area where many different types of plants grow, and nature generally thrives.

The soil from this area, or those helicopter seeds, would make an excellent addition to a money jar. Why? Because this spell is about making money sweet on you. I imagine that you want *lots* of money and adding these elements to your jar translates to an abundance of money coming to you.

As you know by now, it's not just about throwing these into your jar, sealing it shut and then going about your day. You have to speak your intention into everything you're adding to your work. This means telling everything you put inside why you chose it and what you want it to do for you.

For the helicopter seeds, you might say something like: *Money falls in abundance all around me and into my lap. Money surrounds me everywhere I go.* Or *Bring an abundance of money into my life.*

For the soil: *Make my business and my work fertile for all types of money and abundance to grow. Abundance is now well-rooted in my life.*

Let's talk about some of the items on the actual list above. Citrine is considered the 'merchant stone'. It is added to this jar for helping you to make wealth a solid part of your life, and to ensure that the wealth that comes to you is produced through positive means. It's also a great stone for dispelling negative energy.

Bismuth is a stone of transformation, and as such it may not be suitable for your money jar. However, I recommend it if you're looking for any kind of change to your financial situation. It's a stone associated with both the crown and root chakras, and as such can help you ground yourself if you tend to be 'in your head' or feel like you don't belong.

You have to program (speak into) everything before adding it to your jar, but this is especially true for clear quartz. This stone amplifies all energy, so you could add it to your spell as an overall booster.

Instructions

Optional. If you already have tarot cards or a crystal collection, use them to help you build the energy. Use larger crystals like malachite, or tree and moss agate. Likewise, use the tarot cards that speak 'money' to you: Wheel of fortune, ten of cups, ace of pentacles, nine of cups, etc. (Note I've used the Rider Waite names for these cards, but they might have different names in your deck.)

Light the incense and begin your spell using the phases described above.

Run all of the items from your pantry, the crystals, and materials through the smoke. Ask that it all be cleansed of negativity and blessed for your working.

Once everything is cleansed and your prayers have been said, it's time to begin. Start with the dollar bill. Put it on the plate and use the marker to write your name and date of birth. Draw a clockwise circle around it.

Anoint the bill with the honey, and then rub it in. (Taste it first, if you work with Oshun!) While rubbing the bill with the honey, you can say something like: *Money loves me like bees love honey!* You want to speak into each ingredient added to your jar in a similar way.

Once the honey is rubbed in and the bill is charged, put *you* on the bill. Add your hair, some toe or fingernails, speak to the bill. These should stick to the honey and stick to the bill. This is what you want. Feel free to add more honey if you want.

Fold the bill towards yourself at least three times. Once the bill is folded into a small square, use the string to tie it closed. Speak to it one last time, and then add it to the jar.

Now you can start to add the ingredients from your pantry, the crystals, the soil and dirt, or whatever you got from your hood, and the coins. Do not forget to speak what you want as you work.

Feel the energy build.

Work it.

Embody the energy of what you want coming to life.

Once you've added the last item, mix the jar around and let everything sit for a while. You've created a working jar that will sweeten and bring money to you. Speak to the whole jar three more times before closing it.

Set the jar down and place your candle on top. Let the candle burn all the way through, and the spell is complete!

The last step: celebrate! Thank the spirits for their help and for coming to your aid. You can do this while you're cleaning up the space and putting all of your materials away.

As your hoodoo pantry builds, you'll no doubt collect mojo that will add some power to your jar. You can, of course, use what you have--and that is what you are supposed to do as a practitioner, but you may want to wait after gathering a few things.

Common herbs that are widely used in hoodoo, but that you may not have on hand include catnip, alfalfa, and high john the conqueror.

Spells for Success

Success can come to you in different ways for many different aspects of your life. You might want to see more success over yourself, as in, you want self-mastery to accomplish personal goals or remove a habit that no longer serves you.

You may have a specific situation in which you want to be successful, such as a presentation at work or a performance. You may want a success spell for a driver's test or a bar exam.

In each case, you can draw energies towards you, such as focus, or a boost in confidence. On the other hand, you may want to banish some personal trait that is at odds with your goal.

In addition to spells for success (either for specific issues or general), there are many rituals you can use to keep the energy flowing towards you and your home. Holy water is excellent for this. Not only will it clean your space and banish negative entities, but it can also be used to bless. To get holy water, you can go to a botanical or any shop that sells magickal items.

Many herbs can also be used to attract success, such as aloe, basil, bay leaf, and chamomile. These can be mixed and matched with other ingredients to make a success incense.

One of the best things you can do for personal success is to carry and maintain a mojo bag.

Success by Banishment: A Simple Fire Spell

This is a spell that can be done using fire. For this reason, you want to use something that won't release toxic fumes in the air and that you can actually destroy.

Though you do not have to use fire, you can still destroy things with other methods, such as chewing.

While unpleasant, this alternative method involves biting and chewing an object that is charged with the energy you want to banish. For this spell, just remove references to burning and bite and chew instead.

You will need:
1. A banishing incense.
2. An object that you are okay with destroying.
3. A cauldron, fire-resistant dish, or a plate.

To really put the power into this working, try to find an incense that corresponds to what you want to banish. Usually, I would say use what you have, and that applies here as well, but if there isn't anything you have in your home that could be used as an incense, a little shopping might be necessary.

Here are some common examples:
- **Alfalfa** for banishing all forms of poverty from your life.
- **Asafoetida** for banishing negativity (does not smell nice).
- **Black Pepper** for banishing lower energies.
- **Cloves** for banishing hostility and gossip.
- **Curry** for banishing evil.
- **Gravel Root** for banishing discord or tense energies.
- **Peppermint** for banishing illnesses and lower energies.
- **Rosemary** for banishing negative vibrations.

- **Rue**, a popular herb in hoodoo. Burn to banish negative habits and energy.
- **St. John's Wort** for banishing demonic energy.
- **Thyme** for general banishing, specifically negative energies.

Hopefully, you already have one or two items on this list, and if that's the case, you can do this spell today. Provided the moon is in the right phase. As banishing work, this is to be done during a waning moon.

Instructions

Light your incense.

While the smoke rises, take the object and program it for the thing that you want to banish. If you're looking to banish jealousy or envy, asafoetida might be a good option if you can stand the odor, though cloves or rue do not smell as bad and will work as well.

If you can't find an item, get creative with some paper. Write down every detail you can about what you want to banish. Alternatively, you can draw something, or find an image online, print it out, and then add to it anything that helps with conjuring the energy of what you want to banish.

Put into the object all of the energy of the thing you want to banish. Keep speaking it through and talking until you are able to pinpoint the exact energy. This step requires some real focus.

Once you have the object programmed, add you. This can be some of your hair, spit, or toenails, but keep in mind that you will be burning the object.

Carefully light the object on fire and set it in the dish or cauldron. Burn it until all that is left are ashes. For this, make sure your space is well ventilated and you have some open windows. This is for safety and to clear your space of fumes, but it's also to clear your space of the energy you've burned.

You've finished the spell, and the thing you want gone from your life is banished. Success will now come to you swiftly, so the last step is: celebrate.

Success by Invoking: A Simple Candle Spell

Crown of success oil is a widely available conjure oil that can work very well in candle spells for success in any endeavor.

This is a basic candle spell that can be tailored and updated for any type of work you need to do. You will need to change the color of the candle, and the conjure oils you use, but knowing how to do a candle spell like this one will be important for your magickal practice.

You will need:
1. A candle that is wide enough to stand on its own and that you feel comfortable writing in. White candles can be programmed for any use. Otherwise, a color that corresponds to your intent. For example, pink for a health-related spell.
2. Scissors or something sharp to carve with.
3. Crown of success conjure oil.
4. Your intent.

Instructions

Cleanse all of your materials. Carefully carve your name and date of birth into the candle using a sharp end of the scissors (or whatever you have to carve with).

On the opposite side of the candle, or underneath your name, carve in what it is that you want. If your petition is a little long for a candle, try editing it down to a couple words, such as 'dedicated subscribers'.

Anoint your candle with the crown of success oil, making sure to go from the bottom and upwards. Cover the wick, your name, and the petition with your fingers, which should have the oil on them.

Add your essence by speaking your intention into the candle before lighting it. Once it's lit, recite the Psalms and express gratitude. You can also speak to the flame and put into it everything you want.

This is something you want to think about *before* casting your spell: the type of problems that will follow when you achieve. Do you want these problems? Speak your anxieties or worries about achieving success to the fire. Ask Spirit and your ancestors for help with all that will come as your star rises.

Continue burning the candle until it goes out on its own. If you achieve your goal before the candle is finished, you can stop doing the daily ritual. I like to let the candle burn out on its own one last time and use the light as a reminder to keep a gratitude attitude.

If the candle goes out before you achieve what you're looking to achieve, consider the spell complete. Whenever you think about the spell or catch yourself worrying about results, remind yourself that you did the spell and the work is done.

I can understand the temptation to do another spell but do your best to resist doing another working. This will undermine the candle spell you've already done and undermine your magick overall.

You can, however, *continue* the work by anointing yourself with crown of success oil, or burning the oil with an herb in a homemade incense.

When you speak about whatever you cast for, speak as if what you want has already happened, especially if you are speaking to yourself about what you want.

Never think of the spell as having "not worked". (It's fair to say this goes for any spell you do.) If what you wanted did not happen, think of how you can do things better next time. Or better yet, think of how the spell worked in any unexpected ways.

Success by Invoking: A More Complicated Candle Spell

A version of this spell appeared in the first volume of Hoodoo, Conjuration, Witchcraft and Rootwork, by Harry Middleton Hyatt. These volumes feature interviews of the earlier practitioners of hoodoo, and while it can be difficult to understand at times, it contains many spells that were shared among people via word of mouth.

As such, it is a highly valuable resource for anyone who cares to take a look.

This spell is for general success for something time-bound, like a test or if you want someone to pay you back quickly. Before I get into the spell, it requires lighting a perfume on fire, and then lighting a candle with that flame. I cannot control you or what you do, but I have to caution you on this because playing with fire is dangerous.

Last warning: be careful.

You will need:
1. Van van (a perfume).
2. A fire-resistant plate or a cauldron.
3. A lighter.
4. Three green candles.

Instructions

Do this spell on a Monday at 6 in the evening, during the waxing moon.

Put some van van in the fire-resistant plate.

Light the van van so there's a flame inside the plate. Light your first candle, speaking your intention, and let the candle burn until it is complete.

You will be repeating the same process using the second candle on Wednesday (at 9 in the evening). Use the third candle on Friday (at 12 in the afternoon).

Van van oil is another favorite among hoodoo practitioners, so if you end up getting some for this spell, you could use it in other ways for success that do not involve lighting it on fire.

One method is using the oil in floor washes. Adding it to the water you're using to mop with is a simple and effective way to pull in the energy of success into your space. This was reportedly a popular way of using van van among practitioners in New Orleans.

It also works when added to bathwater or for hoodoo baths.

You can also add the oil as a dressing for your candles and leave that on your ancestor or money altar.

Spells for Justice

Generally, when we think of spells for justice, we're thinking of court cases. However, justice applies in many, many areas of life. This is because justice is really about balance.

This is another area where hoodoo was and is very popular among rootworkers, especially in the United States.

These types of spells are also very useful in situations where you have been wronged by someone else, but you're not able to go through legal channels to balance the scales. This might be because going to a court or the police may incriminate yourself, or you want to ensure justice is meted out appropriately.

Many of us are very familiar with the legal system in the states. We also know that going through legal channels can often cause more imbalance, and more problems than it solves.

Luckily, we have hoodoo.

Another dose of realism is important here, as it is in love spells. Before you do any of these spells, you want to get a feeling that your spell has a chance of actually working.

For Court Cases: A Simple Fire Spell

This spell is a version of one from the folks at Yeyeo Botanica.[3] It is best used in smaller court cases, where you may have to appear as a member of a jury, or the issue is relatively minor. This is *not* for major cases where you are r named as a major part of the case.

---

[3] Yeyeo Botanica. (2020, February 19). Court Case Spell - Dismiss | Yeyeo Botanica [Video]. YouTube. https://www.youtube.com/watch?v=6_BMpZnxmK8

Read through the ingredients and description of how to do the spell below, and then ask your ancestors if this spell has a chance of working for your situation. Get all the facts and information you need and use your discernment.

You will need:
- A white 7-day candle (it's better if you can get one specifically for the purpose of your working, in this case, going to court).
- A conjuring oil, again, anything that speaks to your work, but snake oil is a good option, if you can find it from a reputable retailer.
- A copy* of the paperwork for the case.
- A black marker.
- Tobacco.
- A cauldron or plate with tin foil so you can collect ashes.

You may wonder why I'm recommending snake oil for this spell and not a court case or law stay away oil. Court case would work for this spell as well, but as a beginner, I am considering that after you cast this spell, you may have no need for a whole bottle of court case oil. On the other hand, a bottle of snake oil can be used for this and in other workings, like protection for example.

For tobacco, empty out the contents of a cigarette (use one from someone else if you don't smoke yourself). If having cigarettes is triggering for you, purchase a cigar from a local bodega.

While there is a lot you can do with tobacco in hoodoo, when it comes to buying ingredients for this spell, I would recommend *not* going overboard.

Buying a whole pack of cigarettes just for this spell is not the message you want to send to spirit. It suggests you will have a lot in your life that you will need to do similar work on.

Approach this with a beginner's mind and just get what you need.

*You definitely want to use a copy of the court case papers because you will be burning it. Keeping the original will provide you with strong evidence when your magick works!

Instructions

Take the oil and use your fingers to draw a large 'X' through the content of the paper. Go from one corner of the page to the next.

Turn the paper upside down and take out your marker. Write down words that reverse whatever this case is about for you. Use your name and date of birth and continue writing words that oppose what is already on the page.

Avoid writing down anything that you desire. This is banishing magick. Everything you're using (the oil and fire, eventually) is about dissolving this situation. If you put down what you *do* want, you send confusing messages to spirit and risk including those good things within the banishing.

Think about what you want when you celebrate victory; *after* the spell is closed.

You will be coming back to this spell over the course of a specific number of days; generally three or seven. For this reason, you may want to set an alarm on your phone to remind yourself to come back to the spell. The day you start this spell is considered day one.

Dress your candle with the oil (place a few drops in at the top) and the tobacco. Light the candle, picturing the court case removing itself from your life.

Rip off a section of the court document copy. Rip the paper away from you.

You will rip a piece of the paper for each day of the working, so consider how many days you will do the work. Take your piece while leaving enough for each day you plan to work.

Set the paper on fire using the lit candle. Let it burn until the fire goes completely out and all that's left are the ashes.

Once all the paper has been burned, collect the ashes. In the traditional version of this spell, you would go to the courthouse and sprinkle all of the ashes there. If your case will be taking place over an online video conferencing platform, it is still possible to do this step. Remember, this work is about spirit. The correspondences still exist even as our world remains in flux.

If there *is* a courthouse address on your paperwork, use this. If there isn't an address, do a little research online to find a courthouse closest to you, even better if you can find a courthouse nearby where similar cases are handled.

For Personal Use: A Return to Sender Candle Spell

Being scammed is one of those situations that can be put into balance with hoodoo. It is very difficult to get your money back when you've been manipulated or tricked into giving it to someone else.

It will also work for situations where someone has done something to you that you know about but aren't able to remedy legally. For example, a manager at work who manipulates the truth to jeopardize your employment.

Before you take the measure to do a spell, you have to know that *justice is already yours*. You could decide not to move forward with the spell, and this would not change. The spell is an affirmation of this; of what you know already.

Remember that hoodoo is about bringing balance to circumstances. Evening the scales. You may be tempted to do *worse* to them than what they did to you, but keep in mind that the realm of justice is not something that you have to worry about.

You aren't the one who exacts justice on the person or people who have done you wrong, that is spirit's job. As with all spells, this is about appealing to these spirits for work on your behalf.

You will need:
1. A black candle.
2. Van Van Oil.
3. Four Thieves Vinegar.
4. Black salt.
5. A knife or sharp object for carving into the candle.
6. A plate that the dressed candle will burn on.
7. Clover (optional, for incense).

Four Thieves Vinegar is especially good for personal protection, especially from negative people who may want to cause you harm. As such, it can be great for shielding you from people who will use you to dump all of their worries (also known as psychic vampires).

The reason I include Indigo Water as a substitute is that for this spell is because it has a wider variety of uses than the vinegar *and* it can be used to keep negative energies from other people away from you.

It is great for cleansing your home or space, and welcome peaceful energy.

Van Van oil is an all-round key ingredient to have as a hoodoo practitioner, but if you don't have any or can't get access, Olive Oil can work just as well.

The black candle in combination with the black salt here is very much about protective energy, but remember that in magic, white is considered universal when it comes to color magic. If you don't have either candle or salt listed above, you can use a white candle and white salt and program it for your needs. Or, you can use a white candle with black pepper.

Instructions

Your glass of water can sit beside a glass of Four Thieves Vinegar or Indigo Water. Remember that over the duration of the next steps, you want to repeat your intention and what it is you want over and over again.

This spell is about keeping any and all negative energies clear, especially any sent to you by other people. Use specific names if you need to.

A sample incantation: *Every curse, evil eye, jinx, or hex, pack it up and send it back.*

You've called in spirit to help you. As you work you can tell the spirit what's happened and how things have fallen out of balance. Do not worry about speaking "holy", swear, roll your eyes, get emotional. Bring up everything that you want removed from your experience.

Carve an arrow in the candle, pointing up towards the wick. If you're using a tealight candle, a small arrow towards the wick works, or you can use a small piece of paper (such as a cue card) to draw the arrow and point it towards the candle.

Dress your candle with the Van Van oil, drawing the oil upwards, towards the wick.

Place the candle on the plate. Remember, if you need to make sure the candle will stay upright, you can melt the wax on the bottom and stick it to the plate. As the wax cools it will secure the candle.

Now you're going to draw a circle around the candle in a counterclockwise motion. Start at 12 and go around until you've completed the circle. Use enough salt so your circle is clear. I like to neaten the granules so none of the salt is too far off the boundary, and creates a solid barrier around.

Let the candle burn to completion and know that it is done.

Spells for Protection

If you're not used to having a relationship with spirit, one thing you may have heard is that once you've started to open up, you are open to *all* types of relationships. While this is true, it doesn't mean that you are vulnerable.

You decide if you are vulnerable or not. This is the power of your word.

There's a lot you can do to build and maintain a protective shield without an oil or candle. One tactic is surrounding yourself in a shield using your mind.

Much like creating a mental altar, you can create and maintain your aura with the power of visualization and prayer. The effects usually aren't quite immediate, but within a few minutes to an hour after your visualization, you will begin to *feel* protected.

Do not underestimate the power of cleansing when it comes to protection. This is because, as we've discussed previously, energies get attached to us without our knowledge or awareness. These energies can then weaken our fields, which leaves us vulnerable to more harmful spirits.

Cleansing here doesn't always have to be using an incense or Florida Water spritz. Meditation can be a form of cleansing. Same with exercise, showering, and chanting, yelling, or screaming. Simple, daily cleansing (and protection) can be done using the four elements: fire, water, air, and earth.

Sometimes removing those negative entities can be just a matter of screaming it out or putting your frustration on paper (both being examples of how you can cleanse using air).

Many hoodoo practitioners carry something on their person with the intent of providing protection. Usually, it's something small or inconspicuous (if not invisible) that most people who aren't familiar with magick wouldn't associate with anything spiritual.

This could be anything from a prayer, wearing an evil eye amulet necklace, to a mojo bag or nation sack (a type of mojo bag usually carried by women).

For each of these spells, cleansing is very important *prior* to the work. This is because the spells you will be casting are about containing what is already within your home or yourself. So cleanse, cleanse, cleanse, and then get busy.

For Your Home: A Spell Bottle

This is a great spell for overall protection. Though you could create it ahead of specific circumstances that require protection for the home and the people inside. This could be a new neighbor who is proving to be a challenge, or visitors coming in for a short period of time.

In this case, you would do your protection spell before the visitors arrive, and a cleanse after they leave (regardless of how long they're staying for). However, this bottle will continue to work even after your cleanse.

A spell bottle for your home is great you have a lot of random visitors or energy passing by. If you live on a ground floor of a busy street, or you work from home and see patients regularly (whether in person or via online).

Depending on who is visiting and what their energy is like, you might feel the need to double up on protection. In this case you can use a spell bottle and then modify the candle spell above. Remember, in many cases, the simpler a spell, often the more effective it can be.

You will need:
1. A bottle that you can use *just* for this spell. It will not be reused or opened after the spell is cast.
2. Home Blessing oil.
3. Black ribbon.
4. Black candle.
5. Camphor.
6. Angelica.
7. Yarrow Flower.

8. Dragon's Blood.
9. Redbrick dust.
10. Holy water.
11. Frankincense resin (or essential oil).

Get a special bottle specifically for this working. This is one of those 'cast it and forget it' spells. That doesn't mean the spirits will forget about you or the work, but it does mean that you'll rarely (if ever) lay hands on or see the bottle again. So, you don't want to 'miss it'.

One thing you'll often see in hoodoo work is the use of skull and bone curios. This is to recognize the spirits that have come before us and have passed on and can be particularly effective in protective magick.

In this way, it's fortunate that the skull shows up in our daily life so much. It is not rare to find a bottle in the shape of a skull at a local liquor store, or a crystal molded into the shape at a metaphysical store.

While skulls work for many people, this imagery might not be what you want for a protection bottle. I encourage you to get creative with how you work this spell. Think of the bottle itself as being for the spirits you are calling in for your work. You can tie different objects and symbols to it using string or use the ribbon to wrap around the bottle and seal it with candle wax.

If you have trouble thinking of something you can add as a part of the bottle that will speak to spirit, go to your ancestors or the people in your family.

I'm willing to bet there's some image or association you have from childhood or that is relevant to your heritage that you can incorporate into this spell.

Instructions

Use the Holy Water on your hands and sprinkle it around your space. Light the black candle. You will leave it lit until it burns out on its own.

This spell is very simple to do, physically. You are placing each of your ingredients inside the bottle while doing your prayers and incantations.

Start with the heavier ingredients and layer them with the lighter mojo.

Once the spell is complete, find a dark, empty corner of your space and place the bottle there (ideally the bottle is small enough to fit). Whereas in other spells you would do the work every day, with this you *want* to forget that you cast the spell and the bottle exists.

Hiding it is important for this very reason. It's also important that other people--especially children! -do not touch the bottle or open it.

For Your Self: A Loving Protection Oil

As I've said before, a mojo bag is more than enough to provide you with protection on a daily basis.

The spell below is an oil for special circumstances, when you know you're going to be in the vicinity of someone who has trouble when it comes to the concept of *boundaries*. Physical or emotional.

Create this oil at least two weeks before you will be in contact with the person or situation of concern. Then, when you know things are about to go down, use the oil to anoint yourself. (You can use this oil on yourself at any time.)

You can use these oils to simply moisturize your hands. You can anoint candles with it ahead of meditation or prayer. You can pray over the oil and just chill with the spirit of protection.

It does have some romance, with the addition of rose petals. While they are beautiful and inviting, remember: every rose has its thorn.

When it comes to protection magick for the self, I always add at least a pinch of love in.

You will need:
    1. A black candle.
    2. A glass bottle.

3. Cinnamon sticks (you will be using one, make sure it can fit in the glass bottle).
4. Pink salt.
5. Castor oil.
6. Dried rose petals.

Instructions

Another simple spell, for this one we're going to layer the ingredients inside the bottle, starting with the cinnamon stick. You can follow the order above for the rest of the items.

You may also want to use Holy Water for this spell by putting some on your hands and sprinkling it around your space. This is optional.

The one "item" I did not include on this list is *you*. Before putting the cap on your bottle, add something of yourself to the spell. This can be some of your hair, nails, blood, or spit.

I do not consider this to be an ingredient, but if you do, it will make a fifth mojo for this spell. To some, five means change and upheaval, so you may want to consider adding an additional ingredient.

A resin-like Myrrh is both healing and protective, and associated with Mother Mary or the goddess Isis. An essential oil like rosemary can lend both cleansing and protective properties to your oil. It is spiky and has the ability to encourage clarity.

You don't need to add either of these to your bottle; this is where I encourage you to get creative.

As much as you might want to, do not use the oil right away. Let it sit for at least two weeks before using it. Let your work rest in a dark space away from sunlight (a medicine cabinet is perfect).

Part III: Eradication and Getting Professional Help

The Internet has made it possible for people to find out about powerful ways to get revenge and make things happen. Unfortunately, the speed of how we live today has also created this idea that results have to be visible, and they have to be quick.

Things can get out of hand for new hoodoo practitioners who are working without guidance or covering the basics.

News of folks who get wrapped up in working with spirits they have no experience with has made the rounds online, especially lately. These sensational stories trigger curiosity, enthusiasm, hope, and a little fear.

This is not how hoodoo works, most of the time. Often the real-life result is much smaller than those much-talked-about big stories. More than that, the person doing a spell or working experiences consequences they never expected.

One of the dangerous consequences of dabbling in magick without proper training is, in short, making a mess.

You can invite an entity into your life that won't leave, or you can become so obsessed with the work you do, you create a situation that looks and feels like a mental illness (in yourself, not an intended target).

In this case, it might be time to do a thorough eradication, or seek professional assistance.

Unhexing, Banishing, and Eradication Work

At some point as you practice hoodoo, it may be necessary to perform unhexing, banishing, or eradication work. It isn't always the work of someone else that you may have to banish or eradicate.

If you cast a hex on someone else, you will need to unhex yourself. These types of consequences have a short name: karma.

We tend to think karma is synonymous with punishment, but most of the time it is much deeper than that. Thinking fearful thoughts will cause you to feel afraid. This is karma.

Everything you do has a karmic return. Most of the time we don't recognize what the impact is because it happens in the realm of spirit, or deep within our mind.

In other words, feeling fearful often does not show up as karma because most people teach themselves to *accept that consequence*.

Most people don't know that karma follows just from thinking fearful thoughts. Instead, they think feeling fear is normal. And so, when that feeling shows up, they do not associate it with karma. Thus, continuing a karmic cycle.

Karma is *not* killing spiders and then having a spider lay eggs inside of a shoe. Any time you cast a spell, you are leaving yourself open to its impact, even if you do not notice or believe in what it should look like.

This is one of the reasons new practitioners are cautioned before doing any type of left-hand magick; the type of work where you want to do something to an enemy, for example.

What you do for a spell will have an impact on you. If you're buying a certain powder with the intent of doing work on an enemy, you will have them on your mind for much longer than it takes to do the spell. This could lead to creating an obsession, which doesn't hurt the "enemy" at all, it only hurts the person who is obsessed.

Feeling hate in your heart for someone else reduces your capacity to feel love for yourself.

In the same way, doing a hex on someone else means doing a hex on yourself. If you choose to go this route, after you've hexed another person you will have to banish that work immediately to remove it from your energy.

Before hexing another person, you need to decide if the blowback, however small it might be, is worth it.

As you can imagine this kind of work can get tricky. It is done in the shadows, and when it's dark it's not easy to tell what's coming back to you. Most of the time, your own cleansing and protection is sufficient, but there are situations where more work is needed.

I know we talked before about not having anyone else in your life who is open to concepts of magick or hoodoo, and in this case, that might be a good thing. The more people you have in your circle, the more opportunity there is for attracting negative energy.

This is one of the reasons many people shrink their social circles to the size of a dot, but one of the things I have learned on this path is that it's not the other people who are the issue, it's our idea of those people.

So even if you do have a lot of people around you, maybe others who also seem to be powerful, the only thing you have to be concerned about is your *perception* of those people.

I also have to add a caution here about thinking someone else is "more powerful" than you are. It doesn't always need to be someone who is an expert in hoodoo that may be the culprit of some work. We're *all* powerful, each of us given this power in equal measure. The difference lies in how we *use* that power.

Those of us who have more ownership over their power (which is all that is required to use it) are simply doing our work. And most of the time, we are not interested in hurting anyone else. It just does not appeal to us to put so much of our power on anything but making money and living our best lives.

People unknowingly hex each other--and themselves--all the time. Any time you send negative thoughts to someone else, or someone else thinks negatively about you, that is a hex. Add to this repeated thoughts, and that adds more and more energy.

This isn't anything to be afraid of, like I said it happens all the time. You'll go to the grocery store and notice other people in some kind of argument, or some stranger will say something to you, or an incident of road rage happens. The work we've talked about previously, the spells above and mojo bags, are excellent for protection against these kinds of minor disturbances.

These are also often the kinds of attacks on your aura that can turn into something bigger by the amount of energy *you* put into it.

Many people think that every minor offense, or even the suggestion of disrespect, is enough to get them riled up. I know what it's like to be like this, and if you don't, you probably know someone like this.

By now you probably won't be surprised to know that this energy, itself, is in effect a type of hex. We might not know or call it that. We think hexes are about tripping up over life, suffering from bad luck, or living a life of tragedy.

What is a Hex?

A hex is basically anything that is affecting you in a way that stops you from feeling peace.

And there is a very simple way to tell if there is an energy "on" you that needs to be removed: you do not feel peace or you have a very hard time feeling peaceful.

This could show up in your work, where you're having a hard time with coworkers or a manager. Or it might be emotionally, where you've lost motivation for your life. It could be in a relationship, where a once loving and warm space is cold.

Now if there are situations in your life that have been unsettled for a long time, your job is to take a close look to see if the reason behind these issues is something you've caused.

Did you decide at some point that you would never be able to make money doing what you actually love to do? Or did you decide to give up on love?

Most often, the answer here is inside of yourself. An issue in one area of your life is not what a hex makes, the same with minor issues, such as a flat tire or an upstairs neighbor making noise excessively.

Life will do what life does.

How to Know

If you have sudden and strange issues across multiple areas of your life, then you may need to start thinking about the possibility that someone has done work on you. The keywords here are 'sudden and strange'.

While it is true that the work might have been done years ago, if you've been hexed, the issues in your life will feel unusual in some way. It may also be that your regular spiritual self-care doesn't work to alleviate them.

Something always seems to be off; items break or are lost, communication with others always seems like it's happening through a foggy window or broken telephone. It might feel like you are never heard clearly, or that others do not *want* to hear what you have to say.

One place where you will really need to use your awareness is with yourself and with your thinking. Can you focus on completing tasks and go about your day or do you always seem distracted? Do you get confused when trying to figure out simple problems? Do you feel unable to focus? Have your job or employment prospects been affected negatively?

I cannot bring this question up without also talking a bit about mental health; the hot topic of the day. You will know if and when it's time to see a professional, or hopefully you have a network of support around you that can help.

Either way, it can be very difficult to stay neutral and centered if your mind isn't well. There's no way around this; your magick just will not work if your mind is unsettled. Living a life of health *is* living a life of magic.

But you have to do your best to keep yourself in balance. This means doing all of the physical-health stuff that can go neglected without regular maintenance. And it might require seeing a doctor or a therapist.

Don't make the mistake of thinking these activities aren't "magickal"; everything we have here on earth is for our help; not just the plants and roots. This includes the technology and resources, other people who have studied the mind, or who are willing to share their lessons learned. Even our problems all exist *for* us. It all depends on the way you think about it.

Look back at journal entries to see if there's a noted change or difference in what you write or the tone you use. Think over the past few months or years and make a list of any incidents that stand out to you, anything that seems negative and to have happened 'out of nowhere'.

Of course, this would be easier if you've kept detailed diary entries for more than a couple years. If you weren't convinced of keeping a hoodoo diary before, you may be now. Note anything that's happened to you that seemed out of place.

As a beginner, it's highly unlikely that you're going to require any clearing work beyond what you can do yourself. If you *have* gathered the evidence, consulted with your guides and found that you do need some major clearing work, the 3-day eradication ritual below is prescribed.

3-Day Eradication Ritual

This ritual is a complete reset for your spiritual life and practice. The cleansing and protection techniques described above are more for daily or regular use.

As a ritual that is designed to be repeated over at least three days. You need only do this once, but you may feel the need for this kind of ritual every few years, depending on your circumstances.

While the work might be serious, throughout this ritual, I want you to bring lightness, laughter, and joy to this process. On their own, joy and laughter have the power to dispel a lot of negative energy. For this ritual, we are going to use that power. And a little mojo.

That mojo will be in using hot water and herbs to make a spiritual bath.

Often, we hoodoo practitioners assume newbies have access to pots, pans, a bathtub, or be able to go outside to complete a ritual. I will warn you now: this will require you to do some things you've maybe never done before, and could invite looks, questions, if not downright interruption if you live with others.

If you don't think this is something you can do without inviting unwanted questions or comments, consider getting in touch with a professional who can help you do the work more discreetly. I'll discuss more about finding assistance in the next section.

Prior to doing this ritual, you will want to take a "regular" shower. During this shower, speak to the water and imagine your worries and troubles washing down the drain.

This ritual also requires air drying, which is not something most people are accustomed to doing. It is necessary, but some practitioners will forego this step. If you want the full impact of this ritual, do not dry yourself using a towel. You *do* want to set things up in your space so you can sit or stand comfortably.

You will also want to wash and dry all of the clothes or linens you will be using after the ritual. This includes bedsheets and pillowcases, for when it's time to go to sleep. Wearing all white after the ritual is an ideal way to really absorb what it is that you're doing. This is completely optional and completely up to you.

After each bath, wash your tub with saltwater (recipe below). This is a little more than some salt mixed in with some water; you will need to purchase this from a hoodoo shop, get some from the sea (if this is accessible to you), or you can make some. I've included the ingredients for this below. The saltwater is very easy to make; mix all of the ingredients until all of the salt is absorbed into the water.

You will need:
1. Two white candles. You will be using these in the bathroom, so try to get either wider candles that can stand on their own, or holders that you can use in your space comfortably and safely. You'll also be in the bath with these candles burning, so you don't want to put them anywhere where they could fall while you're trying to focus.
2. A basin.
3. A smaller cup that you can use in the bath.
4. Lemon.
5. Sage.
6. Basil.
7. Rosemary.
8. Rue.
9. Florida Water.
10. Hyssop.
11. Angelica.
12. Mint.
13. Patchouli (essential oil is fine).
14. Dill.
15. Eucalyptus.
16. Himalayan Salt.
17. Saltwater.

For saltwater:
1. A pitcher of water (3 to 4 liters).
2. Two rocks.

3. 7 grams Epsom salts.
4. 81 grams table salt.

Instructions

Most of us do not have a bathtub or would prefer not to put all these herbs inside of a full bathtub, so I am going to recommend you fill a large basin with water and put all of the herbs inside.

You will be scooping out water and letting it run down your body thirteen times, so if you need to purchase a basin, get one that is as large as possible to hold the water and the mixture. And try to get something that's pleasing to you or that you *want* to use.

Start with the herbs you have (i.e. Leave out the Florida Water, salt, lemon, and any essential oils you're using).

For Dried Herbs: Mix in a pot on a stove with some water and bring to a gentle simmer while praying and speaking over the pot. Let the herbs cook until fragrant and remove from the heat. Let it cool before continuing.

For Fresh Herbs: Remove the leaves from the stems and mix in the basin with water. Rub the herbs in your hands as the water turns green. Speak and pray as you work the herbs.

Once the herbs have been incorporated into the water, add in the rest of your ingredients.

After they've been mixed, it's time to take your spiritual bath. Take the mixture to your shower and set it down. Light the two candles, on either side of you, and pray over yourself. Recite Psalms 51. Bless yourself, the process, and the spiritual bath you're using.

Get in the tub and stand in the middle. Start to say your prayer and continue to do so for the duration of the ritual. Take your cup and scoop out some of the bath. Pour it over your head, letting the water and herbs wash down from your head to your feet.

Repeat this 13 times, making the same statement each time.

This can be something like: *Remove all obstructions, eradicate all hexing, banish all negativity.*

Picture all obstructions, hexes, and negativity being removed from you as the water drips down into the tub. Get out and chill as your skin air dries.

You don't have to continue repeating your prayers after the bath is finished. You can just sit in silence or meditate.

Once you're ready to move on with your day, end the ritual by closing. You can simply clap once and say: *so be it*.

The leftover water can be used in a few ways; you can include them as a floor wash or as a personal cleansing spray. If you used fresh herbs, take these and leave them as an offering outside. Do not reuse the herbs for your next bath, start fresh each time.

If you feel like you need more cleansing, you can do this bath for more than three days. Seven is often enough for most situations, but some folks will repeat the ritual for 13 days.

After Your Bath

Clean your tub using the saltwater. The energies you've washed away are now sitting in the tub, and you want these to be completely out of your space before the next ritual.

You may notice that following the first day you are already feeling lighter, more focused, and more at peace. This is your confirmation that the spell is working! This leads to the next step: Feeling joy.

Once the ritual is complete, you are now free to live your life in the way you truly want, uninhibited by any work you've done on someone else, or anything someone else may have done to you.

Start to celebrate. There is nothing in your way, especially after your last ritual bath. See the roads in front of you clear and imagine your life unimpeded. *You are unstoppable.* Live an unstoppable life.

Over the course of the ritual, you will use your journal extensively. Record the ingredients you use and the time of month and day when you take your baths. Note the phase of the moon. Following each bath, write down anything that occurred to you while you were pouring the bath over your head.

Magick Mastery

Do not be too anxious to be rid of whatever was troubling you before the ritual. It's now when you have to do your best to not think of whatever the issues were that you were having before. Take on the idea that everything in life happens *for* you and make it as literal as possible.

Really, what you want is to learn to practice neutrality as much as you can. As I've mentioned before, you never want to think of any spell you cast or ritual you do as having "not worked". *Everything* you do works, it's just a matter of knowing *how*.

After your ritual, you'll be in a better place to remain neutral towards your life and circumstances: you are centered. This doesn't mean you're emotionally dead inside, it's quite the opposite.

It means you are better able to notice your emotions and things happening in your life without getting caught up in what's happening. From this position, you can take notes on your experience from a position of clarity.

The more you practice this, the easier it will get. The more you can ask for help from your guides and ancestors, the better you will be able to look at your life and know what's going on.

After the eradication spell, you may discover the ways in which you've given your power away by having an incorrect perception of someone else, or of yourself.

From a place of neutrality, you will also be better able to seek out help, if you need it. This next section on getting professional help is for those circumstances where you require work done that is out of your level of experience, or you need work done with tools that would be inconvenient for you to have.

Know that in most circumstances, you can do work on your own. But as a beginner, you may consider hiring an expert if your work involves outside entities, like a court or legal body.

Spiritual Activities Requiring Professional Help

Unfortunately, it is all too common to be scammed when looking for assistance from hoodoo practitioners. This is one of the reasons it is so important to develop a relationship with yourself and to trust your own instinct.

Before reaching out to any professional, get a clear answer from your guides and your ancestors *first*. If you're not sure of your answer, then the answer is simple: do not hire a professional.

How to Avoid Getting Scammed

If you're online and engaging with spiritually focused content in either the form of videos or on Instagram, you'll soon notice other accounts trying to get in touch with you. They may just follow your account or go so far as to try to send a message saying they can help with whatever you need.

These are scams. Always. Every single time.

You might think it serendipitous that someone contacts you saying they can help with your exact problem, but if you've left a comment on another page with details of your issue (or asking for assistance), whoever messages you saying they can help most likely read that comment and used it to market their services to you.

To be a little fair, this scammer probably did some homework but that doesn't change the facts. Most of the time, if you engage, a scammer will be more concerned about getting paid than they are helping you with your problem.

This is rampant in the spiritual community; however ironic and unfortunate it is.

Real experienced hoodoo practitioners *never* reach out to anyone to offer their services, especially online. (This goes for anyone who offers a service or product that is spiritual in any way, not just hoodoo.) The first and most obvious reason is that they are just too busy with their work and the people who are actually paying them to go out and find new clients.

While this creates a shortage, it also means that people who are desperate for help or answers will keep looking for someone or anyone to hire. This desperation makes it possible for scammers to exist.

The simple antidote: do not be desperate.

This is easier said than done, but there is no way of getting around it. Do not make the mistake of thinking you "need" help. All that does is help you muddle up the energy to resolve whatever your issue is.

Why Hire a Professional

Expertise. The most obvious reason you would hire a professional is to obtain the services of someone who is an expert and knows what they're doing. With this comes the convenience of not having to purchase curios you would only use once.

There are some spells and rituals that you must do for yourself. If you're dealing with a delicate situation where you do not want to risk making an error, consider getting professional help.

Karma. As I mentioned before, any work you do will come back to you in some way. For this reason, you may want to get in touch with an expert who knows exactly how to handle energy when it returns. This doesn't mean you won't be affected by the work at all, but an expert can and will help you to know what to expect after it is complete.

Advanced Eradication. Let's say you did the 3-Day Eradication Ritual described above and you discover through your notes and communication with your ancestors that more work is required to remove a hex.

This is one of the most common reasons many seek the services of a worker. They will be able to help you figure out exactly what is going on and the steps required to treat it.

Education. This book is not the final step in your hoodoo practice. As your reading continues, you'll come across many people who can act as guides and teachers. You can't just hire anyone to mentor you, but some practitioners are available for hire to teach you some specific techniques.

Mentorship is a much more involved relationship that usually evolves with the participation of at least two people.

Clarity. It is *very* easy to get confused as you begin your practice, especially when it comes to hearing the voice of your guides and ancestors, and listening to your intuition. This takes practice, and that practice never really ends. It's for this reason that you may, as you begin to open up to communication, decide to hire a professional to confirm what you're receiving.

There's another caution here, though.

At some point in your journey, consulting experts for clarity becomes redundant. You realize that you spent good money to hear things you already knew. Don't think of the money you spent as "a waste", rather it can provide you with a lesson in learning to trust what you already know.

It's at this point that you understand that seeing someone else for clarity undermines your connection to Divine Truth.

Before Your Appointment

Gather your notes and the information you have so that you can give a thorough overview of what the situation is. The first question the worker will ask you is why you came to see them. You want to have this answer clear and to the point. You also want to know, to an as specific a degree as possible, what work you want them to do for you.

This is not a therapy appointment. The more time you spend explaining and getting emotional, the less time they have to give you their read on what's happening. Approaching your appointment with clarity and focus will bring you resolution much faster.

In addition, if you have an hour and spend most of that time complaining or rehashing everything, you're going to be very disappointed at the end of your session when you're left with lingering questions.

Do not go into the appointment with too much excitement or nervous energy, get as calm and centered as possible.

I would also recommend doing a simple spell to remove negative energy from your aura and get more information on your situation. This work is super simple, all you need is a white candle, glass of water and a white egg (brown can be used, but white is better for this purpose).

Instructions

Light the candle and begin your spell.

Fill the glass with water. You're going to break the egg in the water, so you want the glass large enough so it will hold the egg.

Take the egg and hold it in between your hands to consecrate it. Express some gratitude, as this egg will absorb any negative energy in your aura.

Rest the egg at the top of your head and begin to pray. As you pray, gently roll the egg down your head.

Always go in a downward motion. This is to indicate removing energy. If you were to go up, that would indicate drawing energy towards you.

You can repeat this a few times before going to the next part of your body; begin at your crown and roll down the back of your head and neck, then the sides. Be sure to *lift* the egg off of your skin. Do not roll or draw the egg back up your body.

Then move to your back and arms, then to your chest.

Continue rolling the egg down your body, feeling the negative energy leaving you and being absorbed by the egg. Go over your chest, your hands, your abdomen and hips, legs, knees, making sure to get the front and back of your body as much as possible.

Go all the way down to the tops and the soles of your feet (you will want to move the egg over your palms as well, from your wrist to your fingertips).

Crack the egg and spill the contents inside the glass of water. You can dispose of the shell in compost or just leave it outside.

The egg inside of the water will give you an energetic read on yourself and your situation. You want to look for any cloudiness, bubbles, and blood. Take special note of any shapes or images inside. Seeing faces, symbols, numbers is common. They are things you want to be aware of, even if you don't know what they mean.

If you have at least a month before your appointment, you could do more than one egg cleansing, though I wouldn't recommend doing them too close together. Give it at least three days to a week between each cleansing. Take pictures and notes to help you see the changes over time.

Record whatever you notice with the egg in your journal and keep this information, for yourself and for your appointment. You can even take pictures of it and send it to the professional, so they see your results, provided they say this is okay.

Read the information from the egg with some neutrality. You might not be able to interpret what's going on, so start with just what you can see and what reveals itself to you.

It seems every practitioner has a different way of interpreting what's going on with an egg in water.

Bubbles and cloudy lines inside the water indicate negativity. Some say that bubbles, specifically, indicate negativity that was absorbed by the egg. Others say that cloudiness near the egg yolk shows that the cleansing worked.

Blood on the egg is not a good sign. If you see this on the egg or any spots, get checked out by a physician as soon as you can.

Working with Practitioners

The most important thing with heading into your appointment is to *have an open mind*. You are paying someone else to help you with a situation, denying what they say is like buying food and then throwing it out instead of eating it.

At the same time, even if you have an idea of what work you want done, the practitioner may recommend something completely different. This is why it's important to know what spell you want done, and why.

If there's something of specific concern and they recommend doing a spell different than what you expect, you can ask about what you wanted covered in the spell you chose. They may have a much better recommendation on how to get what you want.

For example, let's say you want to do return-to-sender work on a co-worker. But after hearing your explanation of what's going on, the practitioner recommends doing a spell to ease things between yourself and your manager.

You might ask about the work you want returned, but the practitioner intuits that this situation can actually be remedied with a stronger relationship with your manager. So, in addition to the spell, they give you some homework to cut ties to the situation and clear your way at work.

Take in what they tell you, no matter what it is. After the appointment you can consult with your ancestors and guides if there was anything you were unsure about or want clarity on.

You might be tempted to go back to the practitioner to ask more questions, but here again, I would encourage you to try as much as possible to intuit whatever additional information you need.

Ask, first, before sending an email with a photo, or any message over and above the correspondence you've already had. Be conscious that anything a worker has to do for your situation requires their time, which they should be paid for.

You might have purchased an hour consultation but exchanging money for time is really a crude way of putting a dollar value on what is actually being done.

The work usually takes much longer than that, considering what they receive from their guides about your situation, the follow-up, and any correspondence. Then there are materials they use if they do work on your behalf, the time it takes to do the actual work, and send you a summary.

Many practitioners charge less than what it actually costs to do work. They're not tallying up the time they've spent on your case down to the minute because that would be impossible. Spirit does not work with a timer (at least not one we would understand).

The other key consideration is to approach the work with some enthusiasm. Some people will get frustrated if they're asked to do something by the practitioner. They feel that they hired someone else for a working, and so the 'work' (in every sense of the word) should be done by them.

This is not the way to approach hiring a rootworker.

Your life is ultimately your responsibility, not that of the person you hire. Yes, you've paid them to do the spell, but to carry it forward and to *make it work* (again, in every sense of the word), you need to do your part or be willing to do your part at least.

Look at this as a learning opportunity as well. They may not have the time or resources to teach you everything they know, but they can help you to get to the next phase of your practice if you're willing to take in what they're offering you.

The End: Putting It All Together

We've gone over a lot in these pages: the history of hoodoo, working with spirits in nature, water, place, rootwork, herbs, waters, oils, rituals, when to do work, creating mojo bags, hoodoo lamps.

It's fine to pick up a couple concepts from this book and move on if you find hoodoo is not a practice you want to explore any further.

If, on the other hand, you've read the book from the beginning, you may have notes in many different places and be unsure of where to start. You may have already started your next book on the subject of hoodoo, or a different system entirely.

In this section of the book, we'll go over what your next steps will look like.

Start Communicating

When it comes to magick, your starting point is always the same: with spirit. In this context, that means going back to the beginning of this book and getting the basics solid before moving on to anything else.

I know that you want to get into casting spells now, and that is great, but remember: spellcasting happens all the time. Magick happens all the time.

If you have a specific issue that you want to work on, do not think that you absolutely need to do a spell in order to fix it. Even if you've already done a spell, there's always time to start fresh and revisit your understanding of the situation and what the solution may be.

Use the next spell you're planning to do as an opportunity to get acquainted with the basics of the practice.

You can begin by asking your ancestors and guides for their direction on the spell you want to cast and the situation you are working on. Start speaking to them and ask for their help in guiding you in even the smallest details: the colors used, where to purchase herbs and curios, what type of music to listen to, even the clothes you wear.

This might seem like small details that you have "handled", but if you're not already in communication with your guides, this exercise is about opening up to receiving. This is about knowing there isn't an issue too big or too small for spirit.

Knowing you are led spiritually on the smallest details of your life, you are building faith in the power of spirit, instead of faith in your problems. To reinforce this idea, start your practice by building an altar.

If you need some assistance with understanding the guidance you're receiving, consider trying one or two of the many tools of divination available.

Some hoodoo traditions use bones from animals, such as chickens, but do not feel that you must use this method. Tarot cards, crystals, or beads may be more effective for you and that is fine. Go with what you're comfortable with, or already know.

Get Organized

Another item you want to check off your list as soon as possible: get that notebook. Start recording your spells and work.

Give nature priority in your life. Go through your cabinets and what you have right now in the way of plants, curios, herbs, and roots.

Create a space in your home for the items you have that can be used in a spell or ritual, such as candles, incense holders, crystals, empty glass bottles, and containers. Special plates, dishes, and holders for spells are also important to keep easily available. Labels and Google are your best friends here.

Start looking up magickal correspondences of what you have. If there's something you're not sure of when it comes to magick, look it up! You'll be surprised at the variety and diversity of spells you can find online. While they might not all be hoodoo magick, they probably will help spark your imagination.

If and when you purchase something new for your magick, be sure to bless it before using it in any working, and then add it to your records. You may also want to note when you purchased it, if there's an expiration date, when it was blessed, and the moon cycle it was blessed in.

Hold whatever you've purchased in your hands and open up to the spirit of the item. Note down any feelings or messages you receive intuitively.

You also want to practice this communication with all of the herbs, roots, and items you already have that can serve a spiritual purpose. Your connection with the things in your life are there to serve you.

Remember this when you're going through difficulties or are experiencing confusion. The help you need is very often (if not always) within reach. The communication between yourself and the spirits helping you never stops.

Get Cleaning

Before you begin to practice magic, you may also want to start ritualizing your cleansing practices.

This might involve doing your spiritual cleansing of yourself and your home once every three months, or once a month during the new moon. I highly recommend getting your cleansing and protection rituals solid first, before moving on to doing any other types of work.

For a spiritual cleanse of the home, you want to use new tools; a new mop, broom, rags, and bucket.

Your first spells will (or should be, at least) cleansing and protection, such as a spiritual bath. Do not be too anxious about doing all of the steps and doing them "right". Your first time taking a spiritual bath will feel a little odd, regardless of if you're doing it with the guidance of an advanced practitioner.

This first bath won't be your only one. As you take more, you'll become accustomed to the practice, and will find your rhythm.

Remember there are a number of daily rituals and rites you can use for cleansing and protection. This could include imagining a light of protection surrounding you, using an oil every day, saying prayers, using a Florida Water spray, or doing an egg cleansing once a month. If you haven't already, I highly recommend that you be sure to check my other book called "Prayers and Protection Magick to Destroy Witchcraft; Banish Curses, Negative Energy & Psychic Attacks; Break Spells, Evil Soul Ties & Covenants; Protect & Release Favors" -- as

this book will give you many prayer options to recite and to add to your practice. You can find it at
https://www.amazon.com/dp/B096W6J97R

For this reason, many of the items you purchase for your practice will probably be with the intent of cleansing and protecting yourself and your space.

As effective as all of these tactics are, it's important to not overdo things. If your rituals are making it hard for you to go about daily life, they probably need to be revised.

Remember the rule of going down and going up. If you're removing something or cleansing, you always want to move in a downward motion. For your body, that means down from your head to your feet.

To invoke protection, you would move in the opposite direction (so from your feet to your head).

Get Focused

Cleaning and organizing go a long way towards clearing your mind. Same with taking care of your body. Our body is the channel through which we receive communication from our guides, from spirit, and from our ancestors.

But we have to be good with ourselves to make this channel clear. This means taking care of the channel.

I cannot prescribe what this will look like for you; it's different for everyone. Some people feel good if they go for a walk every day and to sit in direct sunlight. Others need a meat-heavy diet and a jog every morning. And for some, biweekly sessions with a therapist, six glasses of water and dancing every day is enough.

The point is to find what helps you to feel healthy and work every day at keeping your spine straight. This is what will put the power behind your work.

As you move forward with studying hoodoo, I would recommend an approach with going towards what is most interesting to you. If you want to study the cultural and religious origins of modern hoodoo, focus your attention there until you're satiated.

There are endless paths you can go with your study. And things can get confusing if you buy or borrow every book available on the topic so please be very discerning when choosing to follow any teachings by listening to your own intuition.

Keep Going

Many advanced rootworkers have been studying for many, many years. Their practice started when they were young children; before they even knew what the word 'rootworker' meant.

They were lucky to grow up in 'root homes', where mothers, grandparents, uncles, and fathers respected the work. Nearly everyone they knew either had their own spells and techniques or had a reverence for people who did work.

For this reason, their lives are attuned to the practice. It is natural for them to live day-to-day in the omnipresence of spirit, and for this they are incredibly fortunate.

Your upbringing may have looked different than this. Instead of going to graveyards and taking spiritual baths, you may have spent Sundays in church, worshipping a God that you were taught would punish you for having sex before marriage.

Or you may have been raised to be afraid of life, dismissive of nature, and afraid to stand out among your peers.

It is for this reason that when advanced rootworkers try to teach people who have not been raised in the tradition, there seems to be a disconnect on what's considered "the basics" by new and seasoned workers.

Common questions I've heard new practitioners ask are: *How do I dispose of food on my altar? Where do I leave alcohol for my ancestors?* And *What the heck can I use [enter ingredient here] for?*

Advanced practitioners often forget or don't know novice practitioners don't live in homes where they have access to Van Van oil, cascarilla, or Frankincense resin.

I tried to keep this in mind when providing instructions and details for spells. In most cases, if you're buying something for a spell described in this book, that curio or mojo is powerful to use in more than one way. I also tried to use spells and information that would be easily incorporated into your day-to-day.

Whatever regular life looks like for you now or has looked like for you in the past, there is always room for magick. How much depends completely on you.

By now you should have a basis of knowledge with which to start a hoodoo practice as a beginner.

This book might not be enough to turn your home into a 'root home', but it's about starting on the path and knowing that nothing is closed to you regardless of your upbringing. Now you have the basics of what you need to move practice forward.

It's likely that as you study and explore, your magick will incorporate hoodoo and other systems, such as Wicca. You can also check out my other book called "The New Witch's Guide to Modern Witchcraft; Basic Wicca Starter Kit of History, Traditions, Solitary
Practice vs Coven Practice, Modern Day Magick Spells and Rituals with Crystals, Candles, and Herbs" if you choose to learn about Wicca.

Regardless of what other books you read, you will be connected with yourself and your ancestors first. This is the approach I've taken in writing all of my books.

My hope is that as your ability to listen and tune into your guidance deepens, you start to receive information about rituals, practices and direction that come from your guidance.

This is the beauty of this practice, and about being outside one defined system, you will learn to find your way and explore the world of magick available to you.

It starts with your connection to spirit. That is all the mojo you need to make hoodoo happen. And so it be!

Thank you

I want to end this book by sending you so much gratitude by saying thank you for taking the time to learn from my teachings on the subject of Hoodoo. I hold this practice very near and dear to my heart and I am very grateful to have had the opportunity of putting it in book format for all of my fellow practitioners out there. I would love to hear your feedback about the book and how much you enjoyed it. You would be a legend if you could leave the book a review as I read every single review with an open mind and heart. Thank you!

~Glinda Porter

Further Reading

A. (2012). Ancestor Paths: Honoring our Ancestors and Guardian Spirits Through Prayers, Rituals, and Offerings (2nd Edition). Oba Ilari Aladokun.

Clausnitzer, D. (2017). Adorned by Power: The Individualized Experience of the Mojo Bag. Religions, 8(10), 213. https://doi.org/10.3390/rel8100213

The Master Book of Candle Burning: How to Burn Candles for Every Purpose by Original Publications Spiritual Books & Supplies (1998) Paperback. (2021). Henry Gamache.

Hopkinson, N. (2003). Mojo: Conjure Stories. Aspect.

Riva, A. (2021). Powers of the Psalms - 365 Ways To Use Psalms (Occult Books). International Imports.

Teish, L. (1988). Jambalaya: The Natural Woman's Book of Personal Charms and Practical Rituals (Reprint ed.). HarperOne.

www.ingramcontent.com/pod-product-compliance
Lightning Source LLC
Chambersburg PA
CBHW030111240426
43673CB00002B/42